TRADITIONAL BULGARIAN COOKING

Hippocrene is NUMBER ONE in
International Cookbooks

Africa and Oceania
Best of Regional African
    Cooking
Good Food from Australia
Traditional South African
    Cookery

Asia and Near East
Best of Goan Cooking
The Joy of Chinese Cooking
The Art of South Indian
    Cooking
The Art of Persian Cooking
The Art of Israeli Cooking
The Art of Turkish Cooking

Mediterranean
Best of Greek Cuisine
Taste of Malta
A Spanish Family Cookbook

Western Europe
Art of Dutch Cooking
Best of Austrian Cuisine
A Belgian Cookbook
Celtic Cookbook
Traditional Recipes from Old
    England
The Art of Irish Cooking
Traditional Food from Scotland
Traditional Food from Wales

Scandinavia
Best of Scandinavian Cooking
The Best of Finnish Cooking
The Best of Smorgasbord
    Cooking
Good Food from Sweden

Central Europe
All Along the Danube
Bavarian Cooking
Bulgarian Cookbook
The Best of Czech Cooking
The Art of Hungarian Cooking
Polish Heritage Cookery
The Best of Polish Cooking
Old Warsaw Cookbook
Old Polish Traditions
Taste of Romania

Eastern Europe
The Cuisine of Armenia
The Best of Russian Cooking
The Best of Ukrainian Cuisine

Americas
Mayan Cooking
The Honey Cookbook
The Art of Brazilian Cookery
The Art of South American
    Cookery

TRADITIONAL BULGARIAN COOKING

Atanas Slavov

HIPPOCRENE BOOKS
New York

Pronunciation Note

For the pronunciation of the original names of dishes, this book uses:

> **a**, as in far
> **e**, as in let
> **i**, as in lick
> **o**, as in toll
> **oo**, as in look
> **u**, as in luck
> **y**, as in yolk
> **y** (at end of words), as in lucky

Copyright © 1998 Atanas Slavov

For information, address:
HIPPOCRENE BOOKS, INC.
171 Madison Avenue
New York, NY 10016

Library of Congress Cataloging-in-Publication Data
Slavov, Atanas, 1930-
    Bulgarian cookbook / Atanas Slavov.
       p.   cm.
    Includes index.
    ISBN 0-7818-0581-3
    1. Cookery, Bulgarian. 2. Cookery—United States. I. Title.
TX723.5.B8S564   1998
641.59499—dc21   97-39796
                                        CIP

Printed in the United States of America.

Contents

Introduction

Here Is How the Story Goes . . .

Miss Douglas was half dead to begin with.That early Spring morning in 1913, the only ambulance in the high mountain valley town of Samokov was honking through the flood of sheep, shepherds, and braying donkeys headed toward their high mountain pastures for the grazing season. Miss Douglas had hardly arrived from Boston to teach at the local American Girl's School of the US Congregational Mission in Bulgaria, and there she was now, desperately gasping for oxygen in a bouncing jalopy on her way to the local hospital. As she described the accident thirty years later, her bedroom was right above the students' bedrooms in the old monastery building which they were using as a dormitory. The girl students, who had spring fever since who knows when, were giggling and jabbering while gobbling bundle after bundle of green garlic to celebrate the return of the sun, and when sleep finally crept in, their innocent garlic breath penetrated through the cracks in the floor and dangerously upset the chemical balance of Miss Douglas's New England body. So much so that she got arsenic poisoning. Those girls were the victims of a most improper and unhealthful peasant diet, Miss Douglas believed, which the Bulgarians would have to give up if they wanted to enter the civilized world.[1]

Strange and disgusting or not, Bulgarian peasants seemed to be quite healthy those days. At the turn of the century,

---

1 Douglas, Edith L. *The Story of My Life in the Balkans and Turkey.* Typescript in the A.B. Library files.

when population statistics were accurate enough to be com-
pared on a large scale, it turned out that Bulgaria had the
largest number of centenarians per capita among all the
recorded countries. Was it the food? scholars asked themselves. The Russian born Nobel prize winner Ilia Mechnikov
even developed a theory that it was because of the consumption of the local yogurt which, in the high mountain valley
of Samokov, is the richest of all yogurts. At the summer
pastures thereabouts fresh yogurt was so thick that it had to
be cut by a knife! Research established that its rare yeast,
which cleansed the digestive tract in a miraculous way,
couldn't survive long outside that region, and that was the
reason why Samokov yogurt remained practically unknown.
The academician named the agent of this yeast *Bacilicus
bulgaricus*. Of course the whole business was considered
somewhat exotic to the Western European palate, but one
way or another the rare bacillus was introduced to France
and later on into the multimillion dollar Dannon yogurt
industry.

As far as the sheep are concerned, they were like rivers of
wool, like a tidal wave of bells and baas, of bleating and
braying uphill and higher up, above the forest line to the
high-mountain pastures for a good six months before the
whole lot of them boiled over again, over cliff and rock edges
and ran down for the winter. The ratio was ten million sheep
to a nation of six million. And here some more statistics: At
the turn of the century, the natural birth rate was two lambs
per sheep, consequently Bulgaria had five million male lamb
sucklings to dispose of each spring. Only female lambs were
kept for wool, milk, and breeding for the next year. Half of
the excess sucklings were exported to Turkey and Greece.
The other half had to be consumed at home: one suckling
for every two Bulgarians (toothless babies and gaffers in-
cluded); three lambs per family for the St. George feasts in
May at which roasting a lamb was a must! The same routine
took place in the autumn—this time, not only were sucklings

to be butchered, but also old sheep that wouldn't give birth in the Spring.

What I just described is characteristic of the descendants of the proto-Bulgars, which are only part of the present day Bulgarian nation. If we were to take only them into consideration, the Bulgarian culinary tradition would hardly differ from any herding culinary tradition from North Africa to inner Mongolia, and that by itself would hardly explain the longevity we spoke of. The heart of the matter is that the Bulgarian nation is a peculiar blend of pre-Christian proto-Bulgars, Tracians, and Christian Slavs, the old Slavs being a farming ethnic group. At the time when the Ottoman Empire spread from the Crimea in the North to Sudan in the South, and from Persia in the East to Morocco and Hungary in the West, Bulgarian gardeners produced fruits and vegetables for the markets of Adrianopolis, Istanbul, and Izmir, and until the 1930s excelled at the farmer's markets of Vienna, Budapest, and Bucharest. The countryside of present day Bulgaria was practically the vegetable garden of the Ottoman Empire and this was the main and essential Bulgarian contribution to the great Turkish culinary school. Without this influence the Turkish dinner table wouldn't have been any different from the grill or from the *koch-kurban* lamb-soup customs that Turks, Seljuks, Tartars, Kumans, Cherkasians, and Pechenegs brought, wave after wave, since the middle of the first millennium to Asia Minor and the Balkans.

We should point out one final peculiarity of the old Bulgarian diet, which might be as important to deciphering the secret of one-time Bulgar longevity as Miss Douglas's garlic calamity: Wine! At the turn of the century, the deadly phylloxera insect devastated European vineyards. American insect-resistant root stock was introduced and vineyards once again flourished. There was only one problem: the American grape stock could not bring the grape to the old high level of natural sugar as the original European varieties did. That was important because it is the natural sugar of the grape that turns into alchohol before the fermentation kills the alcohol-producing yeast in grape juice. In a word, the newer wines had a much lower natural level of alcohol than before, and needed artificial means to reach a marketable level (by the addition of crystal sugar or even of alcohol). Now the French Bordeaux was known to have reached the highest level of natural alcohol. By sheer chance, a small area of old Bulgarian vineyards from Turkish times on a sandy Danube slope had survived the phylloxera plague, and around the end of the century its wine broke the Bordeaux record in high natural alcohol content. The cellars and casks of the Bulgarian village of Novo Selo that produced this wine held a more resistant bacteria culture than the average ones— just as the Bordeaux cellars did. By the end of the century the Novo Selo red dry *Gumza* won more than eighty international medals without hitting the international market. The limited amount of *Gumza* produced was consumed at home together with all that came from old vineyards along the Danube, from the vineyards of Varna and Pomorie on the Black Sea, and from the vineyards of Assenovgrad and Melnik in the Rodopi Mountain area in the south.

It is worth mentioning here that wine was prohibited by Moslem law in the Turkish tradition of the Ottoman Empire. Although the Bulgars, who built the first Bulgarian kingdom in the seventh century, belonged to the great family of Turkic people, they did not take after Mohamed's teaching as the Seljuks, Turks, and Tartars did. When they built their empire on the Balkans they still held to their shaman beliefs and they were one of the only two Turkic ethnic groups that never became Moslem: the Bulgars took to Christianity, and the Hazars to Judaism. So in addition to keeping the vegetable-growing tradition of the Slavs, they stuck to the 3000-year-old wine-producing tradition of the Tracian, who lived in the Bulgarian kingdom even before the Slavs.

So here are the the elements upon which the Bulgarian people, by way of ethnic fate, built their longevity diet:

whole milk yogurt to cleanse the digestive tract; arsenic-rich garlic to break down the cholesterol; high protein sheep meat to build the body; and high natural alcohol, tannin-rich, red wine to decompose the fat; as well as mountains of fruits and vegetables, like sweet carrots—with fructose which makes cane and beet crystal sugar quite unessential! It looks like a combination that a health-conscious New England teacher of the Puritan tradition might shudder in horror at. Yet what keeps one healthy is not depriving the body of "evil" things, but the balance between rich food and the natural agents that break down what is not good for you.

The Art of Bulgarian Cooking

There is one more thing which is worth adding for the sake of the victims of outrageous diets. The art of cooking is what makes one enjoy life the most, what builds positive feelings about one's own self, and helps men and women boisterously dance through life on their toes. Diet is very important, of course, to nourish us, but the joy of eating involves much more than the products that we devour.

To explain it all would take volumes. Yet it is not hard to put it in a nutshell. The art of cooking rests upon three elements that appeal to three of our senses: it is a combination of the appearance of our food (thus appealing to the eye), its taste (thus appealing to the tongue), and the feel of the food against lips, teeth, and tongue when we chew and swallow (thus appealing to the tactile senses of the pallet). This last element, for many reasons, has been almost entirely forgotten today.

Let us touch very briefly upon the main elements of the art of traditional Bulgarian cooking, which unfortunately are disappearing in the contemporary home and restaurant kitchens of Bulgaria.

Should food look "natural" or "civilized?" The balance between these two options is the basis upon which different culinary schools have developed.

Five million years of eating experience has taught man to recognize in plants and animals the proteins, the fats, the carbohydrates, the minerals, or vitamins he needs to sustain his life.

Of greater importance, though, is man's instinctive ability to make a clear distinction between better and less rewarding options in choosing his food, and this is the point at which the spark of art is ignited. If one is avaricious for proteins for the building of his muscles, the richest food for him is grasshoppers—some 98% of the grasshopper's body is protein. That is obviously much better than the 25% protein content of a buffalo's body. Yet one would have to catch and eat at least 140 grasshoppers each day to stay fit! So much concentrated protein, yet so hard to get! Now consider this! Consider the thunder of a 300-strong buffalo herd stomping through the plains before sunrise! A roaring planet of protein! Writing this down right now I am shaking to the marrow of my bone! The downing of just one bull would ensure protein for a family of three for half a year, or food for 600 tribe members for a day's feast celebrating the beginning of the hunting season. Those thundering rumps! It is this "divine" moment of recognition of a rewarding food that makes the heart start pumping with excitement, the mouth water, stomach acids rise, breath deepen, and the joy of fulfillment shine in the eye. All of this is extremely good for the health of course. It speeds up the tiny invisible body cogs of every physiological function.

It is at this junction of our adventure in food that the art of the natural culinary schools start. According to the Michaelangelos of those "natural" schools, beef should look as "beefy" as possible: round and chunky. Legs should be baked with the bone, they teach, shoulders with the shoulder blades, and ribs with the rib cage. Turnips should look "turnipy;" yogurt—as white as possible; coffee and wine should be full of "bubbles," reminiscent of their preparation process; cheese—with no "bubbles," just smooth and cheesy; fat—greasy.

Excess in the development of this art would sound revolting, as excess always does. Turkish culinary masters developed, through selective breeding, a breed of sheep whose tail was _ the size of its entire body, and it is the tail where sheep fat accumulates. So those tails were served on a flat copper dish, browned on top, hot and quivering, as an aesthetic glorification of abundance. Baked lamb heads were served whole, with their tongues sticking out and their white eyes staring on a heap of rice, ready to be plucked with the fingers. The evolution of molasses and damson cheese brought about the developmnt of *Rahat Locum* (a type of Turkish delight), which was not only sickeningly sweet, but was sprinkled on top with powdered sugar to look even more sugary. The most syrupy sweets were called "elegant lady's belly button" (*kadun giubeck*)," and "the lips of the she-snatcher of men's guts" (*dilber dudagi*), and you most certainly do not want to know what kind of lips exactly they meant in nineteenth-century Istanbul coffee houses. Carbohydrates here, no doubt, had become a Hades of sugar syrup.

The "civilized" culinary school has it the other way around. The experts in this school argue that "the natural" is not elevated. Culture, according to this school, is the measure of one's deviation from the pagan ways. God, it teaches, is against the joy of eating, just as He is against the enjoyment of sex, and special circles in hell are awaiting the guilty ones for either of these sins. We all have witnessed the manifestations of aeshetic deconstruction in every area of our life, and the art of cooking is not spared by this school either. In its final excess, meat doesn't look "revoltingly carnivorous"; it is ground, baked, and served shaped as Paschal breads called, what else, but meatloafs. At Easter children bite off chocolate Easter bunnie's heads (to conceal the vulgarity of chocolate on a Holy day), while real rabbits, beheaded, disemboweled, and cut to pieces are stewed with bay leaves which makes their meat look like dry dates dipped in molasses. Chocolate cakes in the thirties were shaped like little rotten forest logs; piglets were decorated

like righteous parsons sucking on lemon slices; and vegetables were worked upon with surgical instruments to look
like garden flowers.

Bulgarian traditional cooking follows the natural culinary
style without stepping over its classical boundary lines into
the bad habits of voluptuous regalement. A baked leg of
lamb is a leg, but it doesn't quiver under mutton fat for the
natural fatness of mutton to be stressed; nor is it cut into
geometrical ¼-inch slices to look like anything else but a part
of the carcass of an animal. It arouses the appetite with
stimulating natural looks without turning you into the Sir
Tobby of Gargantuas. This trait of the traditional Bulgarian
culinary art illuminates its other two aspects: the way it
tastes, and the way it "chews."

So how should food taste? To the old Bulgarian cooks, the
natural taste of the ingredients, and even more important,
the harmonious flavor of a combination of ingredients
should be stressed. Yogurt is served in a way which brings
out the sourness of its specific bacillus. The taste of bread,
buns, and pastries is underlined by the characteristics of the
leavens, yeasts, and sourdough they are prepared with. In
this line of logic, spices are used to bring out the awareness
of the flavor of a specific dish, but they are never allowed
to go loose on one's tongue so as to totally block out the
natural taste of the ingredients as in some Oriental culinary
styles.

Quite characteristically, the *Imam Bayaldu*, one of the
celestial heights of the Ottoman culinary school to which
traditional Bulgarian cooking belongs, in some of the Turkish restaurants in the US and Europe, is prepared with sugar,
not carrots. This is what many modern Turkish cookbooks
suggest. Yet the recipe for this slightly sweet dish was
established long before beet or cane sugar poured its crystals
over the sultan's empire. The sweetness of *Imam Bayaldu* is
meant to come from the natural sweetness of the combination of onion and carrot fructose. Aside from being more
healthful when prepared this way, it hits the middle of the

pallet instead of the tip of tongue, as crystal sugar does, and lingers on with its slightly sour aftertaste. The "sugar approach" is much sweeter of course, but it is not the divine organic onion-carrot sweetness of this early nineteenth century Ottoman invention to which the Bulgarian traditional school adheres.

The most significant peculiarity of the Bulgarian culinary tradition is the tactile effects of chewing and swallowing of food. For consumers educated in mainstream American cooking of today, it might be hard to clarify the intricacies of this most important point of all in the art of cooking, so we will stick to the basics.

It is a simple matter of fiber. (Remember? The thing that helps protect you from cancer!) Big city Americans live and die without ever tasting a real tomato, although America is the homeland of the tomato. Picked long before their vitamins, fructose, and acids are fully developed, commercially long-lasting shopping center breeds are like plastic baseballs filled with dyed water. Because of too much chemical fertilizer, the fibers of peppers break down when roasted. Ground meat is injected with water, which cannot evaporate entirely as is necessary for most recipes which go beyond the droopy mush served in spongy starch buns as hamburgers. Instead of dicing and cutting carrots, we grate them to save time. Instead of crushing walnuts and releasing their oil to blend harmoniously with other oils in a cold dish, we machine grind them into nothingness. Instead of lightly crushing baked eggplant and fresh garlic, preserving their two complementary fibers, we grind them in the mixer into mush. Snake-style gulping of pulp replaces chewing the countless specific types of fiber that vegetables, meat, fruits, bakeries, and pastries offer.

The Bulgarian culinary tradition (no doubt because it is old fashioned) aestheticizes food, which partially helps one to establish a naturally healthful way of eating and helps balance the unhealthful fluctuations in diet. No food is forbidden because nothing in food is harmful as long as one's culture hasn't phased out, for some supposedly "civilized" reason, other foods that will balance the diet.

Since cooking, at the bottom of it all, is about feeding and health, it might be worth casting one more brief glance at the direct interdependence between overall present-day aesthetic trends and the contradictions in our "civilized" eating styles.

It is a well known fact that fashion designers find it easier to design elegant hanging draperies around a slim body rather than sweating out a dress for a rich female figure. Unfortunately, according to some theories, fat is among the good agents that help the absorption of vitamins; without any fat vitality slumps into depression, and bones become brittle.

Let us go back only sixty years ago when drinking wine was considered a sin. Today we find that alcohol may be one of the best agents in protecting us from excess fat.

Am I really going to be sclerotic after eating hardly anything else but calcium-rich cheese all my life, which made my bones like steel? Not at all. Being the garlic monster of all times, at seventy years of age, my cholesterol is 160.

Furthermore if we consider the eating of spring garlic peasant shoots, as well as pagan Indian shrubs, herbs, and greens as uncivilized, we are just bogged down in our ignorance. Nettles (just one example among many) which are considered hardly more than savagery on this continent, are cooked in ten different ways on the Balkans and in the Near East. Nettles are a food rich in iron, which is essential to blood, and their impressive taste hits the tongue further back in the throat than any of the other edible greens that I know. A culinary jewel with unsurpassed dietary qualities!

One has to enjoy eating everything that his gut tells him to eat in the amounts he feels happy to absorb, if he is careful not to leave anything out of his diet under the presure of day to day vogue, and then he will never die! That at least is the belief behind the Bulgarian art of cooking.

Kitchenware

In order to be able to prepare all the recipes in this cookbook, you will need the following utensils, which are not always found in the common American kitchen:

Rolling pin (used in the preparation of the fillo leaves). A ½ to ¾-inch-thick stick for the rolling out of the dough which should be about 3 to 4 feet long. A broom handle would be fine substitute.

Djezbe (for the boiling of the coffee). A narrow neck, broad-bottomed, copper, 2-ounce coffee pot with a 5 to 6 inch long handle. Commonly found in Oriental and Near Eastern food or souvenir stores.

Havan (for the crushing of fresh spices and nuts). Preferably a hard wood mortar which should be able to hold at least 6 cups. The mortar should come with a wooden pestle.

A couple of *wooden spoons* of different sizes (for the stirring of vegetables). Bulgarian style stews tend to overcook the vegetables which makes them tender and quite easy to break. Metal and plastic spoons could easily make a mess of them. Another thing which is worth noting: a plastic mortar or spatula may need sterilization, something which most certainly one is not told at one's shopping center. Hardwood was the material for kitchenware in the Balkans and in the Near East (box tree, oak, sandalwood, dogwood, walnut wood, cornel-tree), and hardwood does not need sterilization. Aside from the additional fragrance and flavor which hardwood utensils bring to the spices and vegetables that they crush or stir, bacteria or molds cannot survive on their surface.

Kebap Tass (for the steaming and cooling down of rice and meat stews). A classical copper vessel which, unfortunately, nowadays can hardly be found outside of museums and old Near Eastern households. Its walls and vaulted lid are deeply curved (like a car radiator). This gives the vessel a very big cooling off surface, bringing out the flavor of all the ingredients in rice and kebab dishes steaming them inside while preserving their fiber at an optimal level.

APPETIZERS

Traditional Bulgarian appetizers are mainly simple cold cuts and sausages: pasturma,[1] smoked filet, bacon, soodjuk,[2] lookanka,[3] bahoor,[4] nadenitsa[5]. Cheese cuts such as syrene (feta cheese) garnished with paprika and a drop or two of olive oil, and kashkaval (yellow cheese) are appetizers served with wine. Honeycomb pieces are chewed together with their wax, and dried fruits (mainly apricots and prunes), as well as roasted and salted walnuts, peanuts, almonds, and hazelnuts are served as appetizers with grozdova rakiya (grape brandy). Cured black olives with olive oil and onions are the main appetizer served with mastika (ouzo).

Here are some popular appetizers which need special preparation, and are usually enjoyed with alcohol drinks.

---

1 Salted mutton. Legend has it that this Bulgarian appetizer dates from the times of Genghis Khan's raids on Europe. Among the many tribes that joined him were his beloved striking force, the "bulgur of the peoples" (the forefathers of the Bulgars) who could ride for weeks in a row,sleeping and eating on their horses. In preparation for their advance guard missions "the Bulgur" slaughtered old lean sheep, crushed their backbones with mallets, and stored them for the road under the saddle. They were preserved this way for quite some time by the salt of the horse's perspiration, and whenever a slice of meat would show from under the saddle, already soft and tender from the pressure and the rubbing during the trotting, it was cut strip after strip by a knife and consumed without dismounting.

2 Ground beef and pork sausage in thin pig intestines.

3 Spiced ground beef and pork hard salami in beef guts.

4 Pig tripe with rice in pig guts.

5 Spiced lean pork with onions boiled in thin pig intestines.

Mashed Eggplant-Garlic Dip
Cyopoloo

1 big eggplant
1 bell or Italian pepper
1 clove garlic
1 teaspoon salt
2-3 tablespoons chopped fresh parsley
1 tomato
2 tablespoons olive oil
½ lemon
2 tablespoons ground walnuts, optional
1 teaspoon vinegar
10-12 cured black olives, optional

* Roast the eggplant and the pepper over charcoal, or in a hot pan, turning them by the stem until their skin is burned and they become very soft inside.[1]

* When each of them is ready (the pepper will be ready before the eggplant) put them in a pot and cover well for a couple of minutes, so that the skins will be easy to peel off. Peel skins off, cut off the stems and clean out the seeds of the pepper.

* Crush the garlic, salt, and parsley in a mortar with a wooden pestle. Do not turn into a mush!

* Grate the tomato on top, discarding its skin.

---

1 Do not cook them in an oven or (a no-no!) a microwave which will ruin the fiber of the pepper and eggplant (If you do put the eggplant in the oven, pierce the skin in two places with a fork, otherwise it might explode in your face when you are taking it out).

*Add the eggplant and the pepper with the olive oil, and mash the whole thing in the mortar with the pestle.[1] Squeeze the lemon on top, add the ground walnuts and stir with a fork.

*Add the vinegar, stir again with a fork, and arrange the olives on top of the dip immediately before the cyopoloo hits the table. Serve cold.

Serves 4.

Boiled Potatoes with Onions
Kartofy S Look

2 pounds potatoes
2 large onions
1 teaspoon salt
1-2 tablespoons vinegar
2 tablespoons olive oil
12 cured black olives, optional

*Peel potatoes and cut into 1 x ½-inch cubes. Steam until tender[2](15 to 20 minutes).

*Meanwhile cut onions lengthwise into crescents.

*Place potatoes, onions, salt, vinegar, and oil into serving dish. Mix. Decorate on top with black olives.

*This traditional appetizer can be served with plum, grape, and fruit brandy (rakiya).

Serves 6.

---

1 In both cases do not use a mixer or a food processor which will turn the dip into soft mush. This will destroy the fiber of the eggplant, pepper, and tomato which has to be felt by the pallet for full enjoyment.

2 Traditionally the potatoes for this appetizer are boiled.

Fried Eggplant
Purzheny Patladjany

2 pounds eggplant
¼ cup salt
1 cup olive oil

For the garlic sauce:
2 big tomatoes
1-2 cloves garlic
4 teaspoons fresh parsley
1 teaspoon salt
2 tablespoons olive oil

* Cut off eggplant stems and slice eggplants crosswise in ½-inch slices. Salt well on both sides. Let drain for ½ hour. Wash in running water and pat dry with paper towels.

* Heat oil in frying pan to very hot and fry eggplants on both sides until light brown (about 2 minutes on each side). Arrange in serving plate.

For the tomato-garlic sauce:

* Peel tomatoes and finely dice into a bowl.

* Crush garlic, parsley, and salt in mortar. Add to diced tomatoes and mix.

* Heat oil in frying pan to very hot and fry tomato-garlic mixture for 2 to 3 minutes.

* Put into a serving dish for garnishing fried eggplants to taste.

Serves 6.

Fried Zucchini
Purzheny Tikvichky

2 pounds zucchini
2 dashes salt
½ cup flour or cup bread crumbs
1 cup olive oil

For the garlic sauce:
   1-2 cloves garlic, chopped
   1 teaspoon minced fresh dill
   1 dash salt
   1 cup yogurt

* Cut off zucchini stems and slice zucchini crosswise in $^1/_3$-inch slices. Salt lightly on both sides.

* Spread flour in shallow dish. Pat zucchini slices dry with paper towel and dip into flour on both sides. Shake off excess flour.

* Heat oil in frying pan to very hot and fry zucchini on both sides until light brown (about 2 minutes on each side). Arrange on serving plate.

For the garlic sauce:

* Crush garlic, dill, and salt in mortar. Add to yogurt in a bowl and mix. Put into serving dish for garnishing fried zucchini to taste.

Serves 6.

Spiced Thick Yogurt
Kutuk

2 pounds yogurt
1-2 cloves garlic, chopped
1-2 tablespoons minced fresh dill
1 dash salt
1 teaspoon olive oil

* Put yogurt in cheesecloth pouch and hang over sink to drain water from yogurt for 2 to 3 hours.
* Crush garlic, dill, and salt with oil in a mortar into a mush.
* Add mush to thickened yogurt in a bowl and mix thoroughly.

Serves 6.

Feta Cheese Baked in Wax Paper
Pecheno Sirene V Hartiya

1 pound lump of dry feta cheese
4 pinches black pepper
4 teaspoons minced green scallions
1 tablespoon paprika
5 tablespoons butter

* Preheat oven to 400 degrees.
* Cut cheese lump in two, and then each half in two.
* Cut four 6- x 7-inch rectangular sheets of wax paper. Grease them on one side with butter.
* Place a cheese lump on top of each greased side of wax paper pieces. Evenly distribute pepper, scallions, pa-

26

prika, and 1 tablespoon butter on top of cheese. Fold each slice in wax paper.

*Grease a flat pan with remaining 1 tablespoon butter. Place packed cheese slices in, and pour some water on top without covering entirely.

*Place baking pan in oven and bake for 15 to 20 minutes, until wax paper is brown.

*Serve baked cheese in separate dishes, still wrapped in the paper. Unwrap and use as an appetizer served with red dry wine.

Serves 4.

Roe Spread
Tarama Hayver

2 ounces roe

1 slice 1-inch thick white bread (about 2 ounces), optional

3 tablespoons milk, optional

2 cups olive oil

1 ounce soda water

1 onion

½ lemon

*Clean the roe from the ovarian membrane.[1]

*Place in a deep, round-bottomed bowl. (Optional: The roe one might find in New York is often oversalted, so it

---

1 The easiest way is to place the roe membrane on a flat dish, put a knife solidly against one end of the membrane without cutting it, and start pulling the end of the membrane from under the knife. This will leave the roe in the dish.

is advisable to add bread and milk in the bowl.) Crush the roe with a solid wooden spoon until well mixed.

*Start pouring a very thin streak of oil into the roe, continuously beating with the wooden spoon. When the mixture thickens, add a dash of soda water and continue pouring a thin stream of oil while beating. Repeat the process until all the oil is absorbed. This might take a good hour.

*Chop the onion as finely as possible. Mix into the roe.

*Squeeze lemon over it, and mix.

Serves 8.

Salted Bonito
Solen Palamood

1 (6-7-pound) bonito
2 (3-pound) boxes kosher salt
Per serving: 1 red onion per 4 slices (16 chunks)
4 lemons
1 ½-pound loaf dark rye sandwich bread

To salt fish:

*Wash bonito very well under running water, or with a hose if available.

*Consecutively open the gills and pull out all the innards. Using a pair of pliers might be helpful. Find cloaca at about $^1/_3$ body length from the tail of the fish and pour running water in to be sure that nothing stands in its way any more. Wash until there is no trace of blood left.

*Place fish in glass, ceramic, or enamel dish. Fill in abdomen with salt, and cover with salt.

*After at least 12 hours, discard wet salt. Fill and cover fish once more with fresh salt. This is the way to store salted bonito for 1 to 2 months.

To prepare for serving:

*One week before using, wash bonito thoroughly. Cover fish with cold water for two hours, change water and continue changing water every two hours until the saltiness of the water in which the bonito is soaked is acceptable to your taste.

*Tie the bonito by the tail using a secure knot and hang outside to air until there is absolutely no dripping any more (this might take 4 to 5 hours).

To serve:

*Start cutting 1 inch thick slices from the head in the direction of the tail. Cut as many slices as you need for serving, and leave the rest for another occasion. Using a method similar to removing the membrane from the roe (see footnote Roe Spread), place knife against end of skin and pull skin until it is off. Take away backbone and side bones which will leave you with 4 chunks of salted bonito per slice.

*Cut red onions in fine slices. Cut lemons across in ¼-inch slices and then once more in half circles. Arrange in serving dish for everyone to fix their own sandwich.

Serves 3 parties of 4 to 6.

Fried Calf Liver
Purzhen Teleshky Drob

4 onions
½ cup minced fresh parsley
½ cup vinegar
1½-2 pounds calf liver
2 tablespoons salt
½ cup flour
½ cup oil
1 teaspoon black pepper

* Prepare marinade by mixing 2 finely chopped onions, parsley, and vinegar in a flat-bottomed pan.

* Cut the liver into $1/3$-inch slices. Salt them with 2 tablespoons salt, and put them in the marinade for 2 hours in a cool place.

* Take out slices, wash with cold water, and salt with the remaining tablespoons salt.

* Dip each piece in the flour and fry in hot oil for 4 to 5 minutes on each side. Slices should remain juicy, but shouldn't emit blood when cut.

* Put liver aside in serving dish and sprinkle a pinch of black pepper on each slice.

* In the same hot oil fry 2 remaining onions, cut lengthwise into crescents, until light brown. Cover each liver slice with fried onion.

Serves 6.

Fried Brain in Bread Crumbs
Mozuk Pane

2 calf or beef brains
2 tablespoons vinegar
4 cups cold water
2 dashes salt
1 cup bread crumbs
3 eggs
1 tablespoon flour
1 dash paprika
1½ cups oil
2 tablespoons chopped fresh parsley

* Wash brains under cold water. Put 1 tablespoon vinegar in container big enough to hold brains, together with cold water and brains, and soak them for 1 to 2 hours. Wash in cold water for a second time and remove membrane, veins, and any traces of blood.

* Place water, 1 dash salt, and 1 tablespoon vinegar in a saucepan, and bring to boil. Add brains and simmer, uncovered, over medium heat for 20 minutes. Let cool for 30 minutes. Drain and dry with paper towels.

* Slice brains into ½-inch thick pieces crosswise. Lay on paper towels and dredge each piece well in bread crumbs.

* Break eggs into shallow bowl. Add flour, dash of salt, and paprika. Beat lightly with wire whisk.

* Heat oil in frying pan to very hot. Dip each piece of brain into egg mixture and coat as well as possible. Fry until light brown on both sides (about 2 minutes on each side).

* Arrange pieces on platter and sprinkle parsley on top while still hot.

Serves 4 to 6.

SOUPS

Sauerkraut Cold Soup
Armeeva Chorba[1]

¼ sauerkraut cabbage[2]
2 leeks
2½ cups sauerkraut juice
4 tablespoons olive oil
1 teaspoon paprika

* Dice sauerkraut and leeks.

* Add the sauerkraut juice, and add olive oil and paprika.

Serves 4.

---

1 One of the few recipes which has remained in common use in Bulgaria since Roman times. Carts with barrels full of sauerkraut were following the Roman legions, when they were on a fast march, to provide the warriors with vitamins against scurvy.

2 If whole sauerkraut cabbages are not available in your shopping area, get a 1-pound bag of sauerkraut, dice it and put it back in its juice. Add to it the juice of one more bag sauerkraut and ½ cup cold water, along with the leeks, paprika, and olive oil.

Cold Cucumber-Dill Soup
Tarator

2 teaspoons chopped fresh dill
1-2 cloves garlic
½ cup whole walnuts[1]
2 tablespoons olive oil
1 pound organic whole milk yogurt[2]
2 medium seedless cucumbers (½ to 1 pound),
    peeled and grated
1 teaspoon salt

* Put dill, garlic, ¼ cup walnuts, and 1 teaspoon olive oil in a mortar. Crush with the pestle until the contents turn into an even pulp.

* Add the remaining ¼ walnuts and crush them too, this time not all of them turn into a pulp, leaving some small pieces.[3] Put the contents of the mortar into a large serving soup bowl.

* Add the yogurt to the bowl and the remaining 1 tablespoon of olive oil and beat together with a fork or a whisk.

* Add grated cucumbers and salt.

---

1 Mechanically ground walnuts cannot add their walnut oil aroma into the tarator blend. When crushed to a pulp together with the dill, salt, and garlic, the whole walnuts release their oil together with their walnut oil fragrance which is an important element of the taste of the traditional tarator.

2 Stonyfield Farm in the USA offers a 3% to 15% fat yogurt which would be appropriate.

3 Some of the small pieces left are pleasant to chew with your teeth, feel with your tongue, and swallow while having your tarator. The crushing will release most of the walnut oil which will blend into the rest of the ingredients of the tarator and bring out its fascinating flavor.

*Add water according to the thickness of your yogurt. Do not water down the tarator beyond its characteristic consistency of a thick (cream) soup.[1] Mix well.

*Add an additional dash of fresh dill on top and serve.

*Keep refrigerated until serving.

Serves 4 to 6.

Cold Tomato Soup with No Oil
Domatena Soopa

2½ pounds tomatoes

1 onion

¼ cup fresh parsley

2 celery leaves

1 small clove garlic, optional

1 teaspoon black pepper

2 dashes salt

3 eggs

*Peel the tomatoes. Grate thoroughly.

*Mince onion, parsley, celery leaves, and optional garlic. Add together with black pepper and salt. Mix.

*Add 1 cup water.

*Keep refrigerated before serving.

*Hard boil eggs. Dice them, and add to soup.

Serves 8.

---

1   A watery tarator will rob you of its original effect on the pallet.

Potato Cream Soup
Kartofena Krem Soopa

2 carrots
1 onion
½ cup fresh parsley
2 pounds potatoes
3 tablespoons butter
2 cups milk
2 tablespoons flour
2 egg yolks

* Finely cut carrots, onion, parsley, and potatoes.

* Sauté carrots, onions, and parsley in 2 tablespoons butter.

* Put in a kettle, add potatoes, and cover with water. Cook over low heat to boil.

* When vegetables are well cooked take off heat. Mash thoroughly with a wooden spoon, and pass through cullender.

* Bring milk to boil.

* In a separate kettle, brown flour in 1 tablespoon butter. Slowly pour boiling milk into the flour, stirring all the time. Add strained vegetables.

* Put to boil a larger kettle to be used as a water bath for kettle with vegetable-flour mix. Set the whole pot with the vegetables into the boiling water and boil another 10 to 15 minutes, stirring to prevent soup from sticking to the bottom. Take off heat.

* Put egg yolks in a separate bowl. Add 2 to 3 tablespoons soup, stirring vigorously, thinning egg yolks. Add mixture back into soup and stir.

Serves 8.

Lentil Soup
Chorba Ot Leshta

½ pound lentils
4 tablespoons oil
1 big carrot, chopped
1 onion, chopped
2 cloves garlic, minced
½ teaspoon savory
2-3 dashes salt
1-2 tablespoons vinegar

*Cover lentils with 2 cups water, add oil, carrots, and onion.

*Boil for 10 to 15 minutes, until soft. Add garlic, savory, and salt.

*Boil for another 10 to 15 minutes and take off stove.

*Add vinegar to taste.

Serves 6.

Tripe Soup
Shkembe Chorba

2½ pounds beef tripe
2 cups milk
1 teaspoon salt
1-1½ teaspoons crushed black pepper

For spicing to taste after serving:
10 peeled garlic cloves
Pinch of salt
2 tablespoons apple cider vinegar
Dash of black pepper
Dash of paprika

* Put beef tripe in a pressure cooker[1] and almost cover with water. Boil for 15 minutes after the hissing (i.e. the boiling under pressure) starts. Remove lid according to safety instructions, and test a small piece of tripe: it should be chewy but somewhat firm. Discard water.

* Cut tripe into ½- by ½-inch pieces. Put back into pressure cooker, add 7 cups of water and boil under pressure for another 5 minutes.

* Open pressure cooker according to manufacturer's safety instructions, reduce to a light simmer, and start stirring the tripe while pouring the milk at a "string thick" trickle into the pot.

* Add salt and crushed pepper and continue simmering for another 20 minutes in the open cooker, until tripe becomes chewy. Do not overcook!

* While the simmering is taking place, crush the garlic cloves with a pinch of salt in a mortar. Put the mash with

---

1 If boiled in a regular pot the preparing of the tripe soup will take 5 to 6 hours.

the vinegar in a serving dish and season to taste with pepper and paprika.

Serves 8.

Mutton and Innards Soup
Koorban Chorba

1 pound mutton
½ pound lamb liver (or any other kind of innards)
1 big bundle fresh scallions
2 tomatoes
½ cup chopped fresh parsley
½ teaspoon salt
½ teaspoon sweet marjoram

*Boil mutton in 1 gallon of water. Cook, removing froth, until tender, usually at least 1 hour.

*When the meat is well cooked, take it out and cut it into ½- by ½-inch pieces. Put back in the broth to complete cooking. Turn heat and simmer for 1½ to 2 hours, until meat is ready to fall apart.

*Dice liver or innards. Chop scallions and tomatoes and add to broth. Add ½ cup water if needed. Simmer for ½ hour more.

*Take off stove. Add parsley, salt, and sweet marjoram. Stir.

Serves 10 to 12.

Beef Soup[1]
Teleshko Vareno

1½ pounds shin of beef or knuckle of veal with the
  bone
1 teaspoon salt
1 teaspoon whole black peppercorns
1 onion, cut into chunks
½ pound potatoes, cut into chunks
2 carrots, cut into 1-inch slices
1 head of celery,[2] diced
1 tomato, diced
1 parsley root, diced
4 tablespoons butter
½ cup minced fresh parsley

For the garnish:
  2 tablespoons grated horseradish
  1 tablespoon vinegar

* Wash beef well. Cut into small pieces. Put in a 3-quart
  kettle together with bone and cover with water, leaving
  meat ½" under water. Bring to boil and add salt, pepper,
  and onion. Boil at low heat, removing froth.

* When froth is gone take out onion with spoon. Add
  potatoes, carrots, celery, tomato, parsley root, and butter.
  Cover the kettle, and simmer for another hour, until beef
  chunks start falling apart.

* When serving, perk up taste of soup by dashing 1
  teaspoon chopped parsley into soup dishes. Distribute
  meat and pour broth with vegetables on top.

---

1 Veal could be used instead.

2 If your local store doesn't carry heads of celery, try two stalks of
   celery, diced.

*In a separate saucedish mix the horseradish with vinegar for individual garnishing of soup portions.

Serves 8.

Chicken Soup
Pileshka Soopa

1½-pound chicken
5 tablespoons oil
2 onions, chopped
1 teaspoon red pepper
2 dashes salt
1 teaspoon flour

*Cut chicken into pieces and saute in oil. Take out.

*Saute onions. When soft, add red pepper, mix in salt and 1 quart water, and bring to boil.

*Put in meat again and simmer till soft.

*Add ¼ cup water to boil with flour, stirring until flour is mixed thoroughly. Add flour mixture to simmering soup and stir one last time.

Serves 6.

SALADS

Easter Lettuce and Egg Salad
Velikdenska Salata

1-1½-pound lettuce head
1 bundle green scallions
1-2 teaspoons salt (to taste)
1 tablespoon olive oil
½ lemon
6 eggs (1 egg per person)
6 black olives

* Wash, clean, and cut the lettuce and the green scallions to fine shreds.
* Add salt, mix with oil, and squeeze lemon juice over all.
* Add 1 hard-boiled egg, cut lengthwise in quarters, for each person, together with the black olives. Mix.
* This Easter salad is enough to serve as an appetizer for a pint of rakiya (schnapps; plum or grape brandy).

Serves 4 to 6.

Carrot Salad
Salata Ot Morkovy

1 pound carrots
1 pound turnips, optional
1 teaspoon olive oil
1 teaspoon salt
²/₃ small can (4 ounces) tomato paste
1 clove garlic, crushed
½ lemon

* Peel and wash carrots and turnips. Shred them on the largest holes of your grater.
* Add the olive oil, salt, tomato paste, and garlic. Squeeze the lemon on top and mix with a fork.

Serves 4 to 6.

Roast Sweet Red Peppers with Onions
Pecheny Cherveny Peperky S Luk

8 sweet red peppers
2 onions
2 tablespoons olive oil
2 tablespoons vinegar
1 teaspoon salt
1 teaspoon chopped fresh parsley

* Roast the peppers over charcoal or in a hot pan, turning them by the stem until their skin is burned and they become very soft inside.[1] Put them in a pot and cover well for a couple of minutes, so that the skins will be easy to peel off. Peel skins off, cut off the stems, clean out the seeds, and cut the peppers into ½- by 1-inch pieces.
* Cut onions lengthwise into crescents and add to peppers.
* Add oil, vinegar, salt, and parsley. Mix.

Serves 4.

---

1 Do not cook them in an oven or a microwave which will ruin the fiber of the pepper.

Red Vegetable Salad
Chervena Salata

¼ head red cabbage
3 red peppers
3 carrots
1 red onion
3 tablespoons olive oil
3 dashes salt
½ lemon

*Cut the red cabbage into ¼-inch shreds.
*Cut peppers across into ¼-inch circles.
*Shred carrots on the largest holes of your grater.
*Cut onions lengthwise into crescents.
*Put all the vegetables into a large bowl. Add oil and salt and squeeze lemon on top. Mix.

Serves 4.

Cabbage and Carrot Salad
Zele Y Morkovy

¼ head cabbage
6 carrots
3 tablespoons olive oil
3 dashes salt
½ lemon

*Cut the cabbage into ¼" shreds.
*Shred carrots on the largest holes of your grater.

*Put cabbage and carrots into a large bowl. Add oil and salt and squeeze lemon on top. Mix.

Serves 4.

Vegetable Salad with Feta Cheese
Shopska Salata[1]

4 peppers

2 onions

3 tomatoes

2 small cucumbers

¼ cup minced fresh parsley

3 tablespoons olive oil

1 tablespoon vinegar

2 dashes salt

½ pound feta cheese

*Roast the peppers over charcoal or in a hot pan, turning them by the stem until their skin is burned and they become very soft inside.[2] Put them in a pot and cover well for a couple of minutes, so that the skins will be easy to peel off. Peel skins off, cut off the stems, clean out the seeds, and cut peppers into ½- x 1-inch pieces.

*Cut onions lengthwise into crescents and add to peppers.

*Dice tomatoes and cucumbers. Add to peppers and onions.

*Add minced parsley, oil, vinegar, and salt. Mix.

*Sprinkle crushed feta cheese on top.

Serves 4.

---

1   Peasant-style salad from the villages around Sofia.

2   Do not cook them in an oven or a microwave which will ruin the fiber of the pepper.

Letttuce Salad with Mushrooms
Zelena Salata S Guby

1 tablespoon olive oil
½ teaspoon salt
1 tablespoon mustard
1 tablespoon vinegar
1 head Boston lettuce
½ pound mushrooms

*Mix olive oil, salt, mustard, and vinegar in a salad dish.

*Add shredded Boston lettuce and mushrooms cut into ½-inch pieces.

*Mix.

Serves 4.

SAUCES AND DRESSING

Garlic Sauce
Podloochvane

1-2 cloves garlic
1 teaspoon chopped fresh dill
1 pinch salt
1 cup yogurt

* Crush garlic, dill, and salt in mortar.
* Add to yogurt in a bowl and mix. Put into a sauce dish and serve for garnishing fried zucchini or other vegetables, to taste.

Serves 6.

Tomato Garlic Sauce
Podloochen Domaten Sos

2 big tomatoes
1-2 cloves garlic
4 teaspoons chopped fresh parsley
1 teaspoon salt
2 tablespoons olive oil

* Peel tomatoes and dice them in a bowl.
* Crush garlic, parsley, and salt in mortar. Add to diced tomatoes and mix.
* Heat oil in frying pan to very hot and fry tomato mixture for 2 to 3 minutes.
* Put into a sauce dish for garnishing fried eggplants to taste.

Serves 6.

Tomato Allspice Sauce
Domaten Sos Sus Mirudiya

2 tablespoons olive oil
1 onion, chopped
1 tomato, peeled and minced
1 tablespoon flour
½ teaspoon ground black pepper
½ teaspoon ground allspice
¼ cup white wine
2 bay leaves

* Put olive oil in a saucepan, add 3 tablespoons of water, add chopped onion and let simmer until the onions turn glossy.
* Add tomato after mixing it in a spoon of hot water.
* Mix the flour well in 2 tablespoons of warm water before adding to saucepan. Add the black pepper, allspice, wine, and bay leaves. Lightly simmer until the liquid evaporates and the sauce remains in its oil (5 to 7 minutes).

Serves 6.

Tomato Sauce with Black Olives
Anhialska Zapruzhka[1]

4 tomatoes
2 tablespoons oil
1 onion
16 pitted olives
1 tablespoon butter
1 teaspoon salt
10 small anchovies
1 cup chopped fresh parsley

*Peel and chop the tomatoes.

*Mince onion. Heat oil in saucepan, and brown onion for 2 to 3 minutes.

*Add tomatoes and cook until juice evaporates (6 to 7 minutes).

*In a frying pan, sauté the olives with butter for 1 minute. Pour the mixture into the saucepan with the onions and tomatoes. Add salt and stir.

*Garnish (meat or fish serving slices) with one anchovy on top of each slice, and pour hot sauce over. Sprinkle parsley on top before serving.

Serves 6 to 8.

---

1 An old traditional Black Sea Coast sauce rarely found today in Bulgarian restaurants.

Bay Leaf Tomato Sauce
Domaten Sos S Dafinov List

1 lemon
4 tomatoes
1 onion
1 tablespoon butter
1 green pepper, sliced thinly into shreds
2 bay leaves
2 teaspoons salt
1 bunch fresh dill, chopped
16 pitted olives

* Peel lemon and cut into fine slices, removing the seeds. Peel, seed, and dice tomatoes.

* Chop onion. Heat butter in a saucepan and sauté onion until glossy. Add shredded pepper to the onions together with tomatoes, bay leaves, and salt. Cook for 5 minutes.

* Garnish (meat or fish) with dill, lemon slices, and olives, and pour the sauce over.

Serves 6.

Tartar Sauce
Sos Tartar

½ cup oil
1 egg yolk
1 teaspoon mustard
1 teaspoon capers
10 gherkins, chopped
½ cup chopped fresh parsley

*Make a mayonnaise by beating together the oil, egg yolk, and mustard.

*Add capers, gherkins, and parsley. Pour over fish.

Serves 4 to 6.

Vinegar and Garlic
Otset Y Chesun

10 garlic cloves
Pinch of salt
2 tablespoons apple cider vinegar
Pinch of black pepper
Pinch of paprika

*Crush garlic cloves with salt in mortar. Transfer to serving dish. Add vinegar, black pepper, and paprika. Mix.

Serves 8.

Egg-Yogurt Sauce
Sos Sus Yaitsa Y Kiselo Mlyako

3 eggs
1 tablespoon flour
¼ cup yogurt

*Beat eggs in a bowl together with flour and yogurt.

*Continuing to beat, add by teaspoonfuls to stuffed peppers, cabbage leaves, or grape leaves. Keep warm.

Serves 4.

VEGETARIAN DISHES

When it comes to vegetables, the discussion becomes rough.

Cooking vegetables is the point at which the main artistic abilities of a Bulgarian cook are tested. Local tradition has it (with good reason) that there is little harm one could do to a good piece of meat: overdone or bloody inside, a good piece of meat is a good piece of meat! It is, after all, just a matter of a good load of protein. That is not the case with a good vegetable which by itself is hardly worth anything, and it is here that one's culinary skills become apparent. In preparing vegetables the perfect harmony between fiber, taste, and flavor is everything, and how one brings out the fragrances of their ethereal oils, and ferments, and fructose shades by crushing, blending, boiling, frying, mixing, and stirring is a thousand-year-old art.

So here is where the problem lies: How do you do all that with suburban shopping-center vegetables which have no taste, no smell, no color, and do not reflect light? Well, not exactly, but they still have artificial coloring, taste of the chemical fertilizers and preservers that prepared them for the mass market, and smell like plastic bags.

Those shopping centers, mind you, are built upon the soil that gave the tomato to mankind. Today there are hundred of breeds of tomatoes, and each of them features a different combination of acidity, fructose, thickness of skin, density of fiber, and amount of juice in the seed cavities. There are dozens of tomato shades available if you care to look around. Which one will you choose to blend best with the preferred shade of eggplant and carrot so you can put together the perfect slice of *Imam Bayaldu*? Most likely that is a decision you will not get to make. All tomatoes on the mass market are the same kind of tasteless, red baseball. The differences among fruit fibers are hundreds upon hundreds, too. The shopping mall has hardwood golf balls instead—pear- or apple-shaped, it really doesn't matter.

If you ever get into the vegetable section of this book, please do not buy mass market vegetables. You must shop for organic vegetables and fruits, which might cost twice as much, yet that is what you should get if you do not want to just waste your time searching the philosophic stone of alchemists that would turn lead into pure gold. Nothing is going to turn a shopping center tomato into a full-flavored tomato. So, if you don't have organic vegetables in your shopping center go to the nearest farmer's market.

It is a strange thing! Bulgarians have always been very poor. But if I told the poorest among them that the average American buys 66 cent dead tomatoes in a store which offers the best organic tomatoes one can think of for $2, and that $2 dollars are one $\frac{1}{2000}$ part of his monthly salary, that poor Bulgarian, if he survives the shock, will think that I am the biggest liar of all time. He buys 45 cent farmer's tomatoes on a monthly salary of $80. He starves, but once in a blue moon during the summer, he will cook an *Imam Bayaldu* the way it has been cooked in those parts for 200 years, and the stars in the sky will freeze to smell it when he takes it off his wood stove.

Baked Eggplant with Onions
Imam-bayaldu

For the preparation of the eggplant slices:
   3 big long eggplants
   2-3 tablespoons salt

For the eggplant dish:
   ½ cup olive oil
   6 big onions, cut lengthwise into crescents
   6 big carrots, cut into ¼-inch circles
   6-8 cloves garlic, cut into ¼-inch circles
   ½ cup minced fresh parsley
   1 teaspoon salt
   3-4 tomatoes (as needed to cover your baking pan)

Preparation of the eggplant:

* Cut off the stems of the eggplants, then cut them lengthwise in six pieces. Generously salt the white meat of the eggplant slices and let the sour liquid drain for 20 to 30 minutes. Wash with water, lightly squeeze, and pat them dry with a paper towel.

Eggplant dish:

* Preheat oven to 350 degrees.
* Heat ¼ cup of the oil in a deep frying pan and saute the eggplant pieces very lightly about 2 minutes on each side. Arrange slices side by side in a flat baking pan.
* Add ¼ cup oil to the frying pan, and saute the onions, carrots, and garlic for 5 minutes.
* Add parsley and salt, and sauté the mixture for another 3 minutes.

* Cover the eggplant slices in the baking pan with the sauteed onions, carrots, garlic, and parsley.
* Cut the tomatoes in thin ¼-inch-thick round slices and arrange them on top of the eggplant mixture so that the entire dish is covered.
* Pour ¼ cup of water around the pan and bake for 1 hour. Serve each person 3 eggplant slices with a big flat spatula, trying to keep the onions, carrots, and tomatoes intact on top.

Serves 6.

Steamed Potatoes with Butter
Kartofy S Maslo

2 pounds potatoes[1]
4 tablespoons butter
1 teaspoon salt
2 tablespoons chopped fresh parsley, optional

* Steam potatoes in a 2-quart pot for 15 to 25 minutes, until soft. Pour out water from the pot. Add butter and cover for 5 minutes.
* Put in a serving dish. Sprinkle with salt.
* Cover with parsley, if desired.

Serves 4 to 6.

---

1   Optional: 1 pound potatoes, 1 pound carrots.

Baked Vegetarian Vegetables
Posten Gyuvech Na Furna

2 tablespoons olive oil

2 medium onions

½ pound green beans

2 pound potatoes

1 medium eggplant

1 celery root

½ pound carrots

2 peppers

½ pound okra

½ pound green peas

2 tomatoes

2 teaspoons salt

3 ounces tomato paste

1 tablespoon paprika

¼ cup chopped parsley

2 tablespoons butter

* Preheat oven to 350 degrees.

* Put 2 tablespoons of oil with 2 tablespoons water in a saucepan. Add the onions chopped longways into crescents and sauté them.

* Prepare the rest of the vegetables. Remove the ends and strings of the beans and cut them in half. Cut the peeled potatoes, the eggplant and the celery root in 1- x 1-inch pieces. Cut the carrots in ½-inch circles. Seed the peppers and cut them in ½-inch strips. Wash the okra and trim their caps. Discard the peapods.

* Put the onions in a big baking pan. Grate the tomatoes over the onions discarding their skins. Add the vegetables with only 1 cup water and the salt. Mix with a wooden spoon. Cover them with foil. Bake for 1 hour.

*Take the baking dish out and remove the foil. Add the tomato paste, paprika, and parsley. Mix well with a wooden spoon. Add the butter (cut into several pieces around the dish). Put back into the oven and bake for another ½ hour, until the water evaporates.

*In order to test whether the *gyuvech* is ready you must try out a potato. If it is ready to eat—you are ready to serve.

Serves 6.

Okra with Tomatoes
Bamya S Domaty

2-3 onions
3-4 tomatoes
5-6 cloves garlic
4 tablespoons olive oil
2 dashes paprika
¼ cup white wine
2 pounds okra
1 teaspoon salt
¼ cup chopped fresh parsley
1 teaspoon red pepper

*Preheat oven to 350 degrees.

*Dice onions, tomatoes, and garlic, and steam in oil with 2 tablespoons water.

*Add paprika and mix.

*Add wine and ¼ cup water and simmer for 30 minutes.

*Meanwhile wash the okra and trim their caps. Add to onion mixture. Add salt and place in a baking pan.

*Bake for 20 to 30 minutes.
*Sprinkle parsley and red pepper on top.
Serves 6.

Leeks with Prunes
Praz Sus Slivy

¼ cup olive oil

2 pounds leeks

1 carrot

1 tablespoon tomato paste

2-3 teaspoons flour

1½ pounds dry prunes without the pits

2 dashes salt

*Put olive oil in 1-gallon pot. Chop 1 head of leeks, grate the carrot, and sauté until leeks and carrot become soft.

*Add the tomato paste. Sauté for 5 minutes.

*In a separate pot bring ½ cup of water to a boil.

*Sprinkle flour into the sautéed vegetables very slowly while stirring the mixture and then add the ½ cup of hot water.

*Bring to boil. Add the rest of the leeks cut across into 1-inch pieces.

*When leaks become soft, add well-washed prunes. Add salt and simmer for another 10 to 15 minutes, until prunes become soft.

Serves 8.

Nettle Gruel
Koprivena Kasha[1]

2 pounds fresh nettles
1 teaspoon salt
8 tablespoons flour
¼ cup ground walnuts
1 teaspoon paprika, optional
10 tablespoons butter
6 eggs

* Put nettles and salt in a 4-quart kettle of boiling water for 5 minutes. Mash thoroughly with a wooden spoon.

* Thin flour in cold water (about ½ to ¾ cup). Add, together with ground walnuts, to nettles. Boil for another 10 to 15 minutes.

* Pour gruel in a serving dish. (Optional: sprinkle paprika on top)

* Melt 8 tablespoons butter and pour over gruel.

* Fry eggs in remaining 2 tablespoons butter sunnyside up. Serve placing one egg on top of nettles in each dish, and pouring remaining butter from frying pan over each of them.

Serves 6.

---

1 The author has picked and cooked large amounts of good nettles that grow in and around Fredericksville, VA.

Onion Gruel
Luchena Kasha

1 pound of seed onions
1 teaspoon salt, divided
2 pounds large onions
8 tablespoons oil
2 tomatoes, diced
1 clove garlic, minced
1 teaspoon paprika

* Boil whole seed onions in water with ½ teaspoon salt until soft. Take off heat and pour out water.

* Dice large onions and sauté in oil and 4 tablespoons water for 5 minutes.

* Add tomatoes, garlic, paprika and ½ teaspoon salt. Sauté for 10 minutes and add seed onions.

* Mix. Sauté for another 5 to 10 minutes, take off heat, and cover for 10 minutes before serving.

Serves 8.

Navy Beans
Zryal Bob

1 pound navy beans
1 small pepper
3 tomatoes
1 small carrot
2 onions, chopped
½ head of celery, chopped
1 tablespoon paprika
1 tablespoon flour
2-3 dashes salt
3-4 leaves sweet marjoram, minced

* Put beans in a 3-quart pot with cold water to cover and soak overnight.

* Next morning pour water out and fill with fresh water. Boil beans on low heat until soft (could take as much as 1 to 1½ hours).

* As soon as beans start boiling, cut off pepper stem and seed the pepper. Add to beans. Peel tomatoes, dice, and add to the beans. Cut carrot across into ¼-inch circles and add to pot. Add onions, celery head, and paprika. Go on simmering until beans are perfectly soft.

* Thin 1 tablespoon flour with 3 to 4 tablespoons boiling water from bean pot until flour is absolutely smooth. Put back into pot with beans. Keep mix simmering for another 5 minutes, add salt and sprinkle marjoram leaves on top.

Serves 6.

Peppers Stuffed with Rice
Pulneny Piperky S Oriz

10-12 green peppers, well-shaped for stuffing
2 onions
8 tablespoons olive oil
1 teaspoon salt
½ cup minced fresh parsley
½ teaspoon black pepper
½ cup rice
5-6 tomatoes

* Preheat oven to 350 degrees.
* Carefully cut off pepper stems and seed them.
* Chop onions. Sauté with 1 tablespoon olive oil and one tablespoon water. Add salt, parsley, black pepper, and rice. Stir.
* Stuff peppers with mixture, filling no more than ¾ full. Top each pepper with 1 teaspoon oil. Add teaspoons of water until each pepper is full.
* Slice tomatoes into ¼-inch circles. Close pepper tops with a tomato circle.
* Put the rest of the tomatoes at the bottom of a baking pan. Add salt and remaining oil.
* Arrange peppers, tomato caps up, in baking pan. Sprinkle ¼ cup of water on top.
* Bake until rice in peppers is cooked (40 to 50 minutes).

Serves 6.

Stuffed Sauerkraut Cabbage Leaves
Postny Surmy Kiselo Zele

1 medium large sauerkraut cabbage

For the stuffing:
  4 onions
  ¼ cup olive oil
  ¼ cup rice
  3 tomatoes, diced
  1 dash salt
  ½ teaspoon black pepper
  1 dash savory

For the sauce (optional):
  3 eggs
  1 tablespoon flour
  ¼ cup yogurt

* Drain cabbage and separate leaves one by one.

* Chop the onions into very fine pieces. Sauté in olive oil until soft.

* Add rice and tomatoes. Sauté for another 5 minutes. Add ¼ cup hot water. Simmer until rice absorbs water.

* Take off heat. Add salt, black pepper, and savory. Mix.

* Put 1 tablespoon in each cabbage leaf and fold edges of leaf tight around the filling forming a "surma." Arrange the surmas tightly into a cooking pot. Put a flat plate on top of the surmas to prevent them from swimming above water. Pour hot water over plate until surmas are covered. Bring water to boil, then turn down heat to low until all water evaporates and the surmas are left in oil.

For the sauce (optional):

* Beat eggs in a bowl together with flour and yogurt while the surmas cook.

* Add a teaspoon at a time of the surma pot liquid to the yogurt sauce, beating the eggs all the time. Keep warm.
* When the surmas are ready to be taken off the burner, add yogurt sauce to it. Cook for 4 to 5 minutes more, then take off heat.

Serves 4.

Stuffed Grape Leaves
Postny Surmy Lozov List

1½ pound grape leaves

For the stuffing:
* Same as for the stuffed sauerkraut cabbage (see the previous recipe) with the only difference that grape leaves are used instead cabbage leaves, and savory should be replaced with sweet marjoram and a dash of fresh dill.

For the sauce:
* Plain yogurt is preferred instead of egg-yogurt sauce.

PASTA AND RICE

Hominy with Feta Cheese
Kachamak Sus Sirene

1 pound hominy
1 pound feta cheese
2 tablespoons butter
1 tablespoon ground red pepper

* Preheat oven to 400 degrees.
* Put hominy to boil in 1 quart water. Reduce to simmer and stir for 10 minutes until it starts to thicken.
* Very lightly butter the bottom of an 8- x 11-inch baking pan.
* Pour in half of very soft hominy to cover bottom of pan ½ inch deep.
* Crush feta cheese and distribute evenly over hominy layer.
* Pour remaining hominy over cheese layer.
* Bake for 10 to 15 minutes.
* Take out.
* Melt butter in frying pan, add red pepper and sauté for 1 to 2 minutes until pepper turns dark red. Do not burn to dark brown!
* Pour sautéed red pepper and butter as evenly as possible over pan and bake for another 10 to 15 minutes.
* Let cool and somewhat thicken.

Serves 6.

Bulgarian Pasta
Yufka

4 pounds flour (14 cups)
10 eggs
2 tablespoons salt
2 cups milk

*Pour flour on surface for kneading. Dig a hole in the middle and put in eggs, salt, and milk. Make dough. Knead well. Tear balls and spread into thin leaves about 1/16-inch thick.

*Cover table with cloth and spread leaves in the sun to dry out.

*When quite dry cut into 2 inch shreds, and then into ½-inch shreds across.

*Put out in the sun to dry thoroughly, or use oven at lowest heat level.

*Store in a cloth bag, or box in a dry place for as long as 1 year.

Bulgarian Pasta with Cheese
Varena Yufka

1 pound yufka (see previous recipe)
1 dash salt
10 tablespoons butter
½ cup diced feta cheese
¼ cup sugar instead, or with, cheese, optional

*Bring 2 cups water to boil. Add yufka and salt, and simmer till soft.

* Rinse with cold water and drain.
* Melt butter and add to yufka.
* Add cheese. Mix.
* Optional: Add sugar to taste.

Serves 6.

Baked Macaroni
Makarony Na Furna

1 teaspoon salt
1 pound macaroni
8 tablespoons butter
½ cup diced feta cheese
4 eggs
2 cups milk
1 cup sugar

* Combine salt with 3 cups water and boil. Add macaroni and simmer until soft. Rinse with cold water and drain.
* Place in a baking dish with lightly buttered bottom. Sprinkle pieces of butter and cheese on top.
* Beat eggs, milk, and sugar and pour on top of macaroni.
* Preheat oven to 400 degrees F. Bake until top of macaroni turns red.

Serves 6 to 8.

Rice Pilaf
Pilaff

2 cups rice
3 tablespoons butter
1 teaspoon salt
dash sweet marjoram, optional

* Before cooking, wash rice in large quantities of water until the water us perfectly clear.
* To 6 cups boiling water, add rice, butter, and salt. Lower heat; simmer until water is absorbed (17 to 20 minutes).
* Take the saucepan off the heat, place a piece of paper towel under the cover, and let stand for 20 minutes.
* Add the sweet marjoram if desired. Stir.

Serves 4.

Tomatoes with Rice
Ddomaty S Oriz

4 tablespoons butter
1 onion, chopped
1 clove garlic, minced
3 tomatoes, diced
¼ cup chopped fresh parsley
1 teaspoon minced dill
1½ cups rice, rinsed well and drained
2½ cups water
1 dash paprika
1 teaspoon salt

*Heat butter, and sauté onion and garlic for 3 minutes.

*Add the tomatoes with their liquid, parsley, and dill.

*Add rice, water, paprika, and salt. Bring to boil, reduce heat, simmer until water is absorbed, 17 to 20 minutes.

*Remove from heat, put a paper towel under lid and let rest, covered, for 15 to 20 minutes.

Serves 4-6.

Zucchini with Rice
Tikvichky S Oriz

2 bundles green scallions

2 pounds zucchini

10 tablespoons oil

3 tomatoes

1 tablespoon salt

1¼ cups rice

½ teaspoon black pepper

1 teaspoon minced fresh parsley

1 teaspoon minced fresh dill

*Cut scallions to fine shreds, dice zucchini and simmer for 5 minutes in oil and 4 tablespoons water.

*Skin tomatoes. Dice them and add to mixture. Simmer for another 5 minutes.

*Add ½ cup hot water and salt, and bring to boil.

*Add rice. Boil for 5 minutes and transfer to baking dish. Sprinkle with black pepper, parsley, and dill.

*Preheat oven to 400 degrees F. Bake for 10 minutes, until rice starts to turn red.

Serves 6 to 8.

Leeks with Rice
Praz S Oriz

2 pounds leeks
10 tablespoons oil
1 teaspoon paprika
1 tablespoon tomato paste
1½ cups rice
1 tablespoon salt
½ teaspoon black pepper

* Cut leeks across into 1-inch slices.
* Add 2 tablespoons water to oil. Bring to simmer. Add leeks, paprika, tomato paste, and simmer for 5 minutes.
* Add ½ cup hot water and add rice.
* Add salt. Simmer until rice turns soft. Take off heat and sprinkle with black pepper.

Serves 4 to 6.

Sauerkraut with Rice
Kiselo Zele S Oriz

2 pounds sauerkraut
2 tablespoons flour
10 tablespoons oil
¾ cup rice
½ teaspoon black pepper

* Dice sauerkraut. Boil in ½ cup water.
* Thin flour in 2 tablespoons water. Add to oil, and add all to sauerkraut.

* Bring to boil, and add rice. Simmer for 5 minutes, and spread in a baking dish.
* Preheat oven to 400 degrees F. Bake for 10 minutes, until all water is absorbed. Sprinkle with black pepper.

Serves 6 to 8.

Chicken Liver with Rice
Pileshky Drobcheta S Oriz

1½ cups rice
¼ cup pine nuts
¼ cup raisins
4 tablespoons butter
1 onion, chopped
¼ pound chicken livers
3 cups chicken stock (or water)
1 teaspoon salt
1 teaspoon black pepper

* Wash rice thoroughly.
* Wash and drain pine nuts and raisins.
* Brown 1 tablespoon of the butter in a saucepan, and add pine nuts and onion. Brown until nuts turn golden color.
* Add the liver pieces and cook for 2 to 3 minutes. Add broth (or water), raisins, and salt and pepper.
* In another saucepan melt the remaining 3 tablespoons butter, and add rice. Stir constantly for 15 to 20 minutes at medium heat.
* Pour the contents of the other saucepan over the rice. Mix and boil for 2 minutes. Reduce heat and cook at lowest possible heat until water is absorbed, 15 to 25 minutes.

*Take off heat, put a piece of paper towel under cover, and let it stand for 20 minutes.

Serves 4 to 6.

EGGS and CREPES

Scrambled Eggs with Peppers and Scallions

Burkany Yaytsa S Piperky Y Look

2 medium peppers
2 tomatoes
1 bunch green scallions (6 good shoots)
¼ pound feta cheese
2 tablespoons butter
4 large eggs
1 teaspoon paprika

* Roast peppers on all sides over a charcoal grill or in a hot pan. Put in a tightly covered pot for 10 minutes. Peel skins and discard stems and seeds. Cut into ½ inch slices.

* Peel tomatoes. Discard seeds and loose juice. Dice remaining solid fiber.

* Clean, wash, and cut across green scallions into ¼-inch slices.

* Crumble feta cheese.

* Melt butter in large hot frying pan. Add peppers, tomatoes, and scallions. Turn down heat to simmer. Stir.

* Add cheese. Stir.

* Add eggs and lightly mix together with vegetables and cheese until the mish-mash becomes fluffy. Do not overcook to hardening. When you take scrambled eggs off heat you should be able to distinguish yolk against whites.

* Sprinkle paprika on top.

Serves 4.

Poached Eggs over Yogurt
Podlucheny Yaytsa V Kiselo Mlyako

2 teaspoons fresh dill

2-3 cloves of garlic

¼ cup whole walnuts

1 teaspoon salt

4 tablespoons olive oil

1 pound organic whole milk yogurt

4 eggs

1 tablespoon paprika

* Put dill, garlic, a dash of the walnuts, salt, and 1 teaspoon olive oil in a mortar. Crush with wooden pestle until the contents turn into an even mash.

* Add the rest of the walnuts and crush them too, but not into a mash. Put the contents of the mortar into a large soup bowl.

* Add the yogurt to the bowl together with 2 cups of water and beat together with a fork or a whisk.

* Bring water to boil in a separate pot. Carefully break one egg at a time, and drop into boiling water, until eggs are evenly white on all sides. Scoop out poached eggs with a big spoon and float in yogurt mix.

* Heat remaining oil in a frying pan, add paprika, and fry for 1 minute. Pour fried paprika evenly on top of floating eggs. Serve yogurt mix with one egg on top in each soup dish.

Serves 4.

Tomato Omelette
Omlet S Domaty

4 tomatoes

8 cloves garlic

3 tablespoons butter

8 eggs

1 teaspoon salt

2 tablespoons chopped fresh parsley

* Boil 2 cups of water and pour over tomatoes in a kettle. Take tomatoes out immediately and peel skins. Remove seeds.

* Dice together with garlic.

* In a frying pan, fry the tomatoes and garlic in the butter. Cool a little.

* Beat eggs in a separate bowl, add tomatoes with garlic, salt, and parsley. Mix. Fry in a big frying pan for 1 to 2 minutes. When bottom side is ready, turn over, and fry on the other side for 1 to 2 minutes.

* Fold in two and serve on a hot plate.

Serves 4.

Sweetened Bulgarian Crepes
Akatmy S Zahar[1]

3½ cups flour
1¼ cups milk
1 envelope dry yeast
½ teaspoon salt
1 tablespoon sugar
12 tablespoons butter, melted
1 cup yogurt or ¼ cup honey, optional

* Thin 1¾ cups of the flour with warm (110 to 115 degree) milk. Add yeast, salt, and sugar.

* Mix thoroughly and knead dough. Cover and let it rise in a warm place. Add remaining 1¾ cups flour, and ¾ cup milk. Leave this dough for 25 minutes in a warm place, covered.

* Heat a large greased frying pan and drop in 1 tablespoon of dough at a time to fry on both sides.

* Arrange the *akatmy* in a baking pan, sprinkling melted butter, and ¼ cup water between them and on top of them. Preheat oven to 400 degrees F. Bake for 8 to 10 minutes. Take out and serve, covering with honey or with yogurt.

* Quite often, instead of honey or yogurt, the *akatmy* are eaten hot with cold ayran[2] drink on the side.

Serves 6.

---

1 This is the oldest known medieval Bulgarian pastry which is still being prepared in the countryside.
2 See *Aryan* (Cold Yogurt Drink) in *Soft Drinks* chapter, page 188.

Crepes with Honey and Walnuts
Palachinky S Med Y Orehy

For the crepes:
   5 eggs
   10 tablespoons flour
   2 cups milk
   1 tablespoon sugar
   1 dash salt
   2 tablespoons butter

For the garnishing and filling:
   8 tablespoons ground walnuts
   8 teaspoons honey
   2 tablespoons powdered sugar

* Beat the eggs well. Gradually add flour without stopping the beating. Pour in cold milk, continuing to stir until the mixture turns into smooth creamy liquid. Add salt and sugar. Mix.

* Heat frying pan. Butter bottom, repeating the buttering, after each crepe is done.

* Pour the crepe mixture into the hot frying pan, and immediately start tilting pan to all sides to make sure mixture evenly covers the entire bottom of the pan.

* Add some butter around edges of crepe with a teaspoon, and turn over to fry crepe on the other side. Repeat process again and again until the whole mix is used.

* Put a tablespoon of walnuts in the middle of each crepe, add a teaspoon of honey, and fold into a roll. Arrange crepes in a large serving plate and sprinkle powdered sugar on top of them.

Serves 8.

Crepes with Chicken Livers
Palachinnki S Pileshky Drobcheta

For the crepes:
   5 eggs
   10 tablespoons flour
   2 cups milk
   1 tablespoon sugar
   1 dash salt
   2 tablespoons butter

For the filling:
   4 tablespoons butter
   ½ onion, chopped
   1 pound chicken livers, chopped
   3 tablespoons chopped fresh parsley
   1 dash salt
   1 teaspoon black pepper

* Beat the eggs. Gradually add flour without stopping the beating. Gradually pour in cold milk, continuing to stir until the mixture turns into smooth creamy liquid. Add sugar and salt. Mix.

* Heat frying pan and butter bottom, repeating the buttering after each crepe is done.

* Pour the crepe mixture into the hot frying pan, and instantly start tilting it to all sides to make sure mixture evenly covers the entire bottom of the pan. Add butter around edges of crepe, and turn over to fry it on the other side. Repeat process until the whole mix is used for the crepes.

For the filling:

* Heat butter and sauté onions.

* Add liver and sauté for 2 minutes.

* Add parsley, salt, and black pepper together with 1 tablespoon water. Sauté for another 5 minutes, until water evaporates.
* Put a tablespoon of filling in the middle of each crepe, and fold into a roll.

Serves 4 to 6.

MEAT DISHES

Mixed Vegetables with Beef
Toorlyoo Gyuvech[1]

1 pound potatoes

½ pound green beans

½ pound okra

½ pound carrots

2 Italian (or bell) peppers

½ pound green peas

1 celery root

1 medium eggplant

2 tablespoons olive oil

1½ pounds beef[2]

2 teaspoons salt

2 medium onions

3 ounces tomato paste

2 tablespoons paprika

¼ cup chopped parsley

2 tablespoons butter

4 tomatoes

*Put aside in cold water cut and trimmed vegetables until the time comes to add them to sautéed meat and onions: potatoes (cut into 1½-inch pieces), beans (remove ends and strings and cut in half), okra (with trimmed caps), carrots (cut crosswise into ½-inch circles), Italian peppers (seeded and cut into ½-inch strips), peas, celery root (cut into 1-inch cubes) and eggplant (cut into 2-inch cubes).

1 The *tyoorlyoo gyuvech* is the richest and most colorful Bulgarian traditional dish which is known to have contained 15 vegetable and meat ingredients. We are giving here a more practical recipe that Bulgarian gourmet fans use nowadays.

2 Usually beef top chuck with the bones. You can use mutton instead of beef.

*Heat 2 tablespoons of oil in a saucepan. Cut meat into 1-inch pieces. Add to oil with 1 tablespoon of salt and 2 tablespoons warm water and sauté for 5 minutes. Remove meat from pan. Chop onions lengthwise into crescents and sauté for 2 to 3 minutes, until they look glazed.

*Put the meat and onions in a big baking pan. Grate one of the tomatoes over them, discarding its skin.

*Drain the vegetables and add to meat in with ½ cup of water and the rest of the salt. Mix with a wooden spoon. Cover with aluminum foil. Preheat over to 350 degrees F. Bake for 1 hour.

*Take the baking dish out of oven and remove the foil. Add the tomato paste, paprika, and the parsley. Mix well with a wooden spoon. Add the butter (cut into several pieces around the dish). Cut the tomatoes into ¼-inch thick circles and lay them on the contents of the baking dish. Return to the oven and bake for another 30 minutes.

*To test whether the *gyuvech* is ready you must try out a potato from under the tomatoes. If it is cooked through, you are ready to serve.

Serves 6 to 8.

Eggplant Ground Beef Soufflé
Mussaka

For the eggplant:
3-4 large eggplants
2 ounces salt
½ cup olive oil

For the mussaka:
3-3½ pounds ground beef
3 medium onions, finely chopped
1 clove garlic, finely chopped
1 medium carrot, grated
½ medium tomato, diced
1 teaspoon black pepper
½ cup minced fresh parsley
1 teaspoon salt
1 pinch dry celery powder
1 dash thyme
1 pinch pine nuts, optional
4 tomatoes, optional

For the souffle:
4 tablespoons flour
1½ cups whole milk yogurt[1]
4 large eggs
1 pinch salt

To prepare the eggplant slices:
* Cut eggplants lengthwise in ¼-inch thick slices. Salt on both sides and put in a separate dish for ½ hour to drain

---

1 The best choice seems to be 13% fat "Stonyfield Farm" organic yogurt.

away the bitter juice of the eggplants. Wash with water and pat dry with paper towels. Half fry on both sides for 1½ to 2 minutes in 2 tablespoons of hot oil. Add 1 tablespoon of oil in frying pan each time you add new eggplant slices to fry. Place slices between layers of paper towels to absorb excess oil.

To bake the mussaka:

* Fry ground meat in same frying pan in remaining oil. Add onions and garlic, carrot, and tomato, stirring occasionally until all the water is out and the ground meat is white. Add black pepper, parsley, salt, celery, thyme, and pine nuts at the end of the frying, mix and take off the burner.

* Lightly grease a 10- x 14- x 3-inch soufflé dish and arrange a layer of eggplant slices to cover bottom. Cover with half of the meat mixture. Smooth out and cover with a second layer of eggplant slices. Cover with the rest of the meat, and again cover with the remaining eggplant slices.

Optional:

* Cover the last layer of eggplant slices with a layer of ¼-inch-thick tomato slices.

* Preheat oven to 350 degrees F. Bake for 45 to 55 minutes.[1]

For the soufflé:

* In a separate bowl mix the flour with yogurt, stirring vigorously until all flour lumps are diluted. Add eggs and mix well. Add a pinch of salt and spread souffle evenly on top of the hot mussaka.

* Raise oven heat to 400 degrees F. Bake for 25 to 30 minutes, until the souffle turns golden.

Serves 8.

---

1   At this point of the preparing of mussaka, American supermarket ground meat will leave you with a baking pan swimming in juice. Discard the juice before covering with the souffle.

Pork with Sauerkraut
Svinsko Sus Kiselo Zele

2 pounds pork, cut in 1- x 1-inch chunks
1 tablespoon paprika
1 whole (3-pound) sauerkraut cabbage[1]
10 tablespoons butter or lard
1 small hot pepper
¼ cup sauerkraut juice mixed with ½ cup water

* Season meat chunks with half of paprika.

* Cut sauerkraut cabbage into thin strips. Put ½-inch layer of sauerkraut with 3 to 4 small butter pieces on the bottom of a cooking pot. Add a layer of pork chunks; continue layering sauerkraut with butter then pork chunks, finishing with a layer of sauerkraut on top.

* Sprinkle top with remaining paprika and the hot pepper cut in two. Add remaining butter cut into small pieces. Pour the mixture of water and sauerkraut juice over everything.

* Bring to a boil, then simmer on low heat for 1½ hours, mixing once or twice, until meat chunks are tender.

Serves 6.

---

1 If whole sauerkraut cabbages are not available in your shopping area, get a 1 pound bag of sauerkraut and a 2 pound fresh cabbage. Chop cabbage and mix together.

Baked Pork and Sauerkraut
Svinsko Sus Zele Na Furna

*If you prefer a baked dish, the pork with sauerkraut should be prepared the same way as above, except before chopping the sauerkraut cabbage you should put aside the three biggest leaves which are on the outside of the cabbage.

*When you place everything in a baking dish, instead of a cooking pot, cover the pork and sauerkraut mixture with the three cabbage leaves.

*Preheat oven to 350 degrees F. Bake for 1 to 2 hours, without mixing, until meat chunks are tender.

Serves 6.

Mutton with Rice
Ovneshko S Oriz

3 pounds mutton
1 teaspoon salt
1 teaspoon black pepper
½ cup rice
12 tablespoons butter
½ teaspoon cinnamon
½ teaspoon pine nuts

*Cut mutton into 1-inch pieces. Salt, cover with black pepper, and put in cooking pot.

*Mix rice with melted butter, cinnamon, and pine nuts. Add to meat.

* Add ½ cup water. Cover very tight. Traditionally the lid was glued to the pot with soft dough to keep the steam inside.
* Simmer for 4 hours.

Serves 6.

Roasted Leg of Lamb
Pechen Agneshky Boot

1 5-6-pound leg of lamb
½ pound seed onions
1 teaspoon salt
1 tablespoon butter
8-16 onces yogurt
1 6-ounce can tomato paste

* Take off excess fat and skin from the leg of lamb. Place in saucepan with seed onions, salt, and enough water to cover. Cook, removing froth, until tender about 60 minutes. Remove from saucepan and place in a baking pan.
* Melt butter, and mix with yogurt and tomato paste.
* Preheat oven to 400 degrees F.
* Spread the yogurt mixture on the meat and roast until crisp, 50 to 60 minutes.
* Suggested vegetables for garnishing: green peas, potatoes, or carrots with butter.[1]

Serves 6 to 8.

---

1 See under Vegetables

Stuffed Lamb Shoulder
Pulnena Agheshka Pleshka

1 pound lamb innards (including lung, intestines, liver)

2 bundles fresh scallions (12-16 shoots)

3 tablespoons butter

1 dash salt

1 cup rice

1 teaspoon chopped spearmint

1 tablespoon crushed black pepper

1 lamb shoulder with the ribs (3-4 pounds)

2 tablespoons salt (for the walls of the pouch of the stuffing)

1 tablespoon paprika

* Bring 3 cups water in cooking pot to boil. Add innards, bring water to simmer, and cook for 30 to 45 minutes. Take innards out and dice them. Discard water.

* Chop scallions, sauté in same pot with 2 tablespoons butter and dash of salt for 5 to 6 minutes. Add innards and 2 tablespoons water, and sauté for another 7 to 8 minutes until innards remain almost entirely in butter.

* Add rice, spearmint, black pepper, and ½ cup water and simmer for 10 minutes.

* Open the shoulder between the meat and the ribs with a knife. Lightly salt the walls of the pouch you just opened with 2 tablespoons salt. Stuff with rice mixture, and sew up tightly.

* Melt remaining 1 tablespoon butter and mix with paprika. Butter shoulder with the mixture.

* Place lamb shoulder in baking pan. Pour water up to the middle of the lamb shoulder.

* Preheat oven to 350 degrees F. Bake for 45 to 60 minutes, pouring sauce from the pan over the meat with a spoon every 15 minutes (until skin of meat turns golden brown, and meat lets out pure water when pierced with a knife).

Serves 8 to 10.

Veal Stew
Teleshko Zadusheno

1 pound veal

2 carrots

4 onions

1 celery root

1 teaspoon salt

4 big potatoes, optional garnish

* Cut veal in 1-inch pieces. Cut carrots, onions, and celery into quarters.

* Cook veal, vegetables, and salt at low heat in 4 cups water, removing froth while water is boiling. When meat stock is clean of froth, cover and cook for 2 hours at low heat.

* If you wish, 1½ hours after the veal has been cooking, add skinned potatoes cut into 1- x 1½-inch pieces and cook together for about 30 minutes until tender.

Serves 4

Sautéed Lamb
Tas Kebab

1 tablespoon butter
2 pounds lamb meat
1 onion, chopped
1 tablespoon tomato sauce
1 tablespoon flour
1 teaspoon salt
2 tomatoes, peeled and seeded

Spice bag of:
  2 cloves garlic
  1 tablespoon thyme
  2 bay leaves
  ½ teaspoon red pepper
  1 bunch parsley

* Heat butter in saucepan. Cut meat into 1-inch pieces and sauté in butter for 6 to 7 minutes, mixing.

* Add onions and sauté for 2 minutes. Add tomato sauce and stir. Slowly add flour, stirring constantly.

* Add 2 cups water, salt, and spice bag. Cook for 15 minutes on low heat.

* Add tomatoes. Cover saucepan. Cook for another 25 to 30 minutes at low heat, until most of the liquid is evaporated.

* Take off heat and remove spice bag.

Serves 4.

Mutton Baked in Wax Paper
Knizhen Kebap

2 pounds mutton
4 tablespoons butter
10-12 bundles green scallions, minced
½ cup chopped fresh parsley
4 peppers, chopped
2 dashes sweet marjoram
½ teaspoon salt
1 teaspoon black pepper

* Cut the mutton into 1- x ½-inch pieces. Sauté in butter, stirring until meat turns white on all sides, 5 to 10 minutes.
* Add scallions, parsley, peppers, and sweet marjoram. Sauté 2 more minutes.
* Take off heat and mix with salt and black pepper.
* Cut six 8- x 8-inch rectangular sheets of wax paper. Lightly grease them on one side with butter.
* Distribute equal amounts of mutton mixture on top of each greased side of wax paper. Fold in sides of wax paper.
* Place mutton packages mutton in a greased pan and pour ½ cup of water on top.
* Preheat oven to 400 degrees F. Place baking pan in oven and bake for 40 to 45 minutes, until wax paper is dark brown.
* Serve contents of each mutton "package" in a separate dish.

Serves 6.

Mutton with Green Almonds[1]
Ovneshko S Zeleny Bademy

For the almonds:
> 1½ cups green almonds[2] (55 to 65 almonds)
> 3 tablespoons salt

For the stew:
> 3 pounds mutton (as lean as possible)
> 3 tablespoons butter
> 1 bundle fresh scallions (12-16 medium shoots)
> 1 clove garlic
> 1 teaspoon salt
> ½ teaspoon spearmint
> ¼ cup chopped fresh parsley
> 1 dash paprika

*Boil almonds in 3 cups water with salt for 10 minutes. Discard water.

*Cut mutton into 1- x 1½-inch pieces. Sauté in butter for 6 to 7 minutes on all sides. Take out meat.

*Chop scallions and garlic, and sauté in the same butter for 2 to 3 minutes.

*Add meat to scallions with 1 cup water, salt, spearmint, parsley, and paprika. Bring water to boil, stir, turn heat down to simmer, cover and cook under lid for 35 to 45 minutes, until most of liquid is evaporated.

*Serve, taking care that each serving has 8-10 almonds.

Serves 6 to 8.

---

1 Traditionally done with suckling lamb this Southeastern Bulgarian classic could be cooked with lean veal as well.

2 The almonds should be picked in the first days of May (depending on the region) when the pit has not yet formed a distinctive shell and the green skin is already quite thick and shows some juice when cut.

Veal with Seed Onions
Teleshky Chumlek

2 pounds veal[1]
¼ cup oil
2 onions, chopped
1 tablespoon flour
1 teaspoon salt
1 teaspoon black peppercorns, crudely crushed
2-3 bay leaves
2½ pounds seed onions
¼ cup red wine
10 cloves garlic, peeled
3 tomatoes, diced
6-ounce can tomato paste
1 teaspoon paprika

* Cut meat into 1-inch pieces. Sauté in 2 tablespoons oil with 2 tablespoons water in a saucepan.

* Remove the meat and sauté the onions in the same saucepan. Mix in flour. Add ½ cup hot water and bring to boil. Add meat, salt, black pepper, and the bay leaves.

* Meanwhile, in a separate pot, boil seed onions, changing their water twice. Drain water. Boil seed onions lightly for another 5 minutes in the remaining 2 tablespoons oil with the wine, adding garlic, tomatoes, tomato paste, and paprika. Add to the meat.

* Simmer at low heat for another 5 to 10 minutes until most of the liquid is evaporated.

Serves 4-6.

---

1 Beef could be used instead of veal.

Stuffed Sauerkraut Cabbage Leaves with Pork
Surmy Kiselo Zele[1]

3 large savoy cabbages

5 pounds ground pork

1 teaspoon ground black pepper

1 dash salt

4 pounds cut sauerkraut leaves

Optional:

2 finely chopped leeks

3 tablespoons oil

1 teaspoon paprika

1/2 cup rice

*Cut out the hearts of the cabbages. Place one of the cabbages on the net of a pressure cooker with the cut-opening down. Pour in 1 cup water and pressure cook for 2 minutes. Open pressure cooker and peel off the soft leaves of the cooked cabbage that are on top. Put them aside and put the rest of the cabbage back into the pressure cooker, repeating the process until the leaves of the entire cabbage are peeled off. Do the same with the other 2 cabbages. Pour remaining water in separate container.

*Cook ground pork at low temperature, separating lumps and mixing until meat turns white. Add the pepper and the salt.

Optional:

*Sauté leeks in oil. Add paprika and rice. Add to the meat and mix well.

---

1 Use the pressure cooker if whole sauerkraut cabbages are not available. If whole sauerkraut cabbage is at hand, use whole leaves after washing them well to remove the salt.

* Put a layer of the toughest (outside) leaves of the cabbages at the bottom of the pressure cooker. Sprinkle a thin layer of cut sauerkraut on top of the cabbage leaves, saving the the juice of the sauerkraut.

* Set aside another layer of cut whole leaves to be used as the top layer. Cut the rest of the cooked cabbage leaves in 4x4-inch squares. Put 2 tablespoons of the meat mixture on in each cabbage leaf, or as much as it can hold. Roll the meat, turning in the edges of the leaf and pressing it tightly in your palm. Arrange the stuffed leaves tightly against each other at the bottom of the pressure cooker. After the layer is finished, cover the stuffed cabbage leaves with a second layer of chopped sauerkraut leaves. Repeat the process of interchanging layers of cut sauerkraut with stuffed cabbage leaves until the stuffed leaves are finished. Cover with chopped sauerkraut, and put a cover of whole cabbage leaves on top. Put a big plate facing down on top of it all to press the stuffed leaves and pour ½ cup of the reserved sauerkraut juice on top.

* Cook under pressure in the pressure cooker for 10 to 20 minutes according to manufacturer's safety instructions. Open the pressure cooker and simmer until the water in the cooker evaporates.

* Let stuffed leaves cool off (without allowing them to turn cold), take out and serve.

Serves 10.

Fried Hamburgers
Purzheny Kyufteta

1 slice bread without crust
2 eggs
1 teaspoon salt
½ teaspoon ground black pepper
½ teaspoon cumin
2 onions, minced
½ cup chopped fresh parsley
2 pounds ground lamb
1 pound ground beef
4 teaspoons flour
1 tablespoon butter

*Soak the bread in water, and when thoroughly soaked, remove from water and squeeze out liquid. Place in a big bowl.

*Add eggs, salt, pepper, cumin, onions, parsley, ¼ cup water, and meat. Knead and roll under your hand, then pat in your palm to shape 3-inch-wide by 1-inch-thick hamburgers.

*Turn over hamburgers one by one in flour, and shake off excess flour.

*Fry them in butter for 5 to 6 minutes each.

Serves 8.

GRILL

Grilled Rissoles
Kebapcheta

3 pounds ground mutton[1]
1 teaspoon salt
½ teaspoon ground black pepper
½ teaspoon cumin
1 onion, minced

* Knead meat and put in a glass or enamel pan spreading it no more than 3 inches thick. Leave under wet cloth in the refrigerator for 24 hours.

* Take cloth off and mix well, adding salt, pepper, cumin, onion, and ¼ cup water.

* Knead and roll under your hand until evenly mixed, then roll in your palm the thickness and the length of a pointing finger.

* Grill on charcoal for 5 to 6 minutes or more on both sides to taste. If the fat of a kebapche catches fire, put the fire out with a good dash of cold water. Turn over and over until ready (rare to well done).

Serves 8.

---

1   Other kinds of meat will do if not too lean.

Hamburgers
Kyufteta

1 slice bread without crust
2 eggs
1 teaspoon salt
½ teaspoon ground black pepper
½ teaspoon cumin
2 onions, minced
½ cup chopped fresh parsley
2 pounds ground lamb
1 pound ground beef

* Soak the bread in water, and when thoroughly soaked, remove from water and squeeze out liquid. Place in a big bowl.

* Add eggs, salt, pepper, cumin, onions, parsley, ¼ cup water, and meat. Knead and roll under your hand until evenly mixed. Put in a glass or an enamel pan, spreading the meat no more than 3 inches thick. Leave under wet cloth for 1 hour.

* Take off cloth and shape into 3-inch-wide by 1-inch-thick hamburgers.

* Grill for 4 to 5 minutes or more on both sides to taste, turning them over and over until they are ready (rare to well done).

Serves 8.

Lamb on Skewer
Shish Kebap

2 pounds lamb (from the thigh or shoulder)
4 tomatoes
2 green peppers
2 onions
1 teaspoon salt
1 teaspoon ground black pepper

*Cut meat in 1- x 1-inch pieces.

*Peel and seed tomatoes and cut into 1- x ½-inch pieces.

*Cut peppers in half, seed, and cut into ½- x ½-inch pieces.

*Cut one onion in half and peel off the round half shells.

*Skewer a piece of meat, tomato, pepper, meat, onion, tomato, meat, pepper, onion consecutively, and repeat until meat is finished.

*Grill, turning on all sides, for 4 to 6 minutes.

*Put in a pot, sprinkle with salt, pepper, and 1 minced onion; cover for 5 minutes to let meat absorb flavors well.

Serves 4 to 6.

Whole Lamb Roasted on Skewer
Pecheno Agne Na Shish

1 fat (12-14 pound) lamb
2-3 tablespoons salt
¼ pound fat

*Disembowel lamb and wash very well under running water.

119

* Salt well inside and out, and sew up the stomach cavity.
* Put on a long wooden skewer in such a way that at least ½ foot of the skewer sticks out on both sides. Place each end of skewer on two forked wooden poles stuck 2 to 3 feet above ground.
* Build a strong twig fire so that its 2-foot flame burns at least 1 foot away from the lamb. Turn the roast all the time, taking care of the fire.
* Attach fat on a long spit. While the turning of the roast goes on (which will take some 3 to 4 hours), be sure to grease the skin of the lamb with the fat, so that the lamb doesn't burn too much.
* Check out whether the lamb is ready to be taken off skewer by putting a fork into the shoulder of the roast. If clean, white juice comes out, lamb is ready to be served.
* Take lamb off skewer, break into big chunks, and find out what Robin Hood's thing was all about.

Serves 20.

Suckling Pig Baked on Skewer
Pecheno Prasentse Na Shish

1 (10-12 pound) suckling pig
2 tablespoons salt
1 tablespoon ground black pepper
2-3 tablespoons tomato paste
¼ pound fat

* Disembowel the pig and wash very well under running water.
* Cover with salt, pepper, and tomato paste all over.

* Stick lengthwise on a skewer, and roast on glowing wood embers.
* Attach fat on a long spit. Turn the roast on all sides, constantly greasing the skin of the pig with the fat on the spit so that the pig doesn't burn too much.
* Check out whether the pig is ready by putting a fork into its shoulder. If white juice come out, pig is ready to serve.
* Take off skewer, and break into big chunks.

Serves 12 to 14.

Grilled Beef Steaks
Govezhdy Purzholy Na Skara

2 pounds beef steaks (4 pieces)
16 tablespoons (2 sticks) butter
1 teaspoon salt
1 teaspoon ground black pepper

* Grease both sides of steaks with soft butter.
* Roast on the grill for 5 to 6 minutes, until brown. Lightly salt, turn over, sprinkle salt, and butter again. Bake the other side until brown.
* Place in serving dish and sprinkle with the rest of the salt and the black pepper.

Serves 4.

Mutton on Skewer
Ovneshko Na Shish

3 pounds mutton
¾ pound bacon
10-15 green peppers
2 teaspoons ground black pepper
2 teaspoons salt
4 onions

* Cut meat into 2- x 1-inch chunks.

* Cut bacon into ¼-inch slices

* Cut peppers in halves.

* Put pieces on skewer in the following pattern: meat, bacon, pepper, meat, bacon, pepper, etc. until all the meat is on the skewer.

* Cover meat chunks with salt and pepper. Grill, turning on all sides.

* Cut onions lengthwise into half moons, and put in a pot.

* When the meat is soft (about 5 to 10 minutes), take off skewer, and place in the pot. Cover with lid and shake. Keep covered for 5 minutes.

Serves 8 to 10.

POULTRY

Hen with Savory
Kokosha Kavurma

3½ to 4-pound hen
2 teaspoons salt
2 onions
10 tablespoons butter
½ teaspoon paprika
6 tablespoons flour
1 shoot dry savory (1 tablespoon if crushed)

* Wash hen well and boil for ½ hour in water with 1½ teaspoons salt. Save the chicken stock.

* Take out hen and break into pieces: legs, wings with the breast, white meat sides in two.

* Chop onions. Stew for 5 to 10 minutes in butter with 2 tablespoons of water, then add hen pieces and paprika.

* Add the stock and bring to simmer. Add flour slowly while stirring vigorously. Add savory and stir. Simmer for 10 to 15 minutes, until meat becomes soft.

* Take off heat and take out savory branch.

Serves 6.

Chicken with Red Pepper
Pille S Cherven Piper

2-pound chicken
1 tablespoon butter
1 onion, chopped
1½ teaspoons tomato sauce
1 tablespoon flour
½ cup white wine
1½ teaspoons red pepper
1 teaspoon salt
1 bay leaf
1½ teaspoons gound pepper
2 cloves
2½ cups chicken broth

*Cut chicken into pieces. Sauté for 5 to 6 minutes in butter.

*Add onions and sauté until glossy.

*Add tomato sauce and flour and stir vigorously.

*Add wine and simmer for another 5 to 6 minutes. Add the rest of the ingredients and stir.

*Cover and cook for 30 minutes at low heat.

Serves 4 to 6.

Roasted Chicken[1]
Pecheno Pile

3-4-pound chicken
2 teaspoons salt
½ cup yogurt
1 tablespoon tomato paste
1 tablespoon butter, melted

* Put the chicken into a saucepan, cover with water, add salt and cook for 30 to 45 minutes, until the meat is quite soft.

* Place the chicken into large pan. Beat yogurt and tomato paste with butter, and cover chicken on all sides with it.

* Preheat oven to 350 degrees F. Roast for 45 to 60 minutes, until tips of wings and legs turn dark brown.

Serves 6 to 8.

---

1 Traditionally served with Rice Pilaf. (See page 82)

Stuffed Chicken
Pulneno Pile

3-4-pound chicken
1 onion
2 tablespoons butter
$1/3$ cup raisins
$1/3$ cup pine nuts
1 cup rice
2 cups chicken broth

* Take bags of innards out of chicken and discard. Take out the livers and dice. Discard the rest. Rinse and drain chicken.

* Chop onion. In a covered saucepan, melt butter and sauté the liver and onion. After 2 to 3 minutes, add raisins and pine nuts. Sauté for 2 to 3 minutes more.

* Add the rice and the chicken broth. Mix. Bring to boil, reduce to simmer, cover the pot, and cook for 15 minutes. Remove from burner, and uncover to cool off.

* Place chicken in a roasting pan on its back. Stuff chicken with rice mixture until two-thirds full. Sew up opening.

* Preheat oven to 350 degrees F. Bake for 1½ hours, moistening chicken with the drippings every 20 minutes. Chicken is roasted when breast is pierced with tip of knife and juice runs clear.

Serves 6 to 8.

Duck with Mushrooms
Patka S Guby

3-pound duck
3 tablespoons butter
2 tomatoes, diced
1½ teaspoons flour
1 teaspoon salt
24 very small onions or shallots
1½ pounds mushrooms
24 large pitted olives, garnish

Spice bag:
1 tablespoon thyme
2 cloves garlic
2 bay leaves
1½ teaspoons peppercorn
½ cup chopped fresh parsley

* Cut the duck into pieces. Sauté the pieces for 8 to 9 minutes in butter.
* Add tomato. Slowly add flour, mixing vigorously. Add salt, ½ cups water, and spice bag. Bring to boil, reduce to simmer, and cook on low heat for 1½ hours.
* Add whole onions and mushrooms cut into 1- x ½-inch pieces, and cook another 20 to 30 minutes. Place duck on warm platter, and pour the tomato mixture over it.
* Garnish with olives.

Serves 6 to 8.

Turkey with Sauerkraut
Puyka Sus Zele

5 to 6-pound turkey

1 celery stalk

1 onion

1 medium (2-2½-pound) cabbage

2 pound sauerkraut, sliced

1 tomato, optional

8 tablespoons butter

1 teaspoon paprika

* Discard innards of turkey. Wash well in running water.

* Put in a big pot and cover with water. Add celery and onion cut in half. Boil for ½ hour, skimming off froth.

* Take out of pot and cut into 8 pieces: 2 legs and 2 wings (with breasts) with the bone, 2 white meat sides divided into 2 chunks. Pick out every piece of remaining meat, discard bones, and save broth with celery and onion.[1]

* Peel off 4 big outside leaves of cabbage and put aside. Cut remaining cabbage into fine shreds. Discard juice of sauerkraut and mix sauerkraut with shredded cabbage. (*Optional:* Mix in diced tomato for a fresher taste.)

* Butter the bottom of a big baking pan. Make a layer of cabbage mix with 4 to 5 small dabs of butter. Arrange the meat on top. Put small pats of butter on the turkey. Cover turkey with remaining cabbage-sauerkraut mixture and pats of butter. Season with paprika, and cover with the 4 big cabbage leaves to protect the cabbage mixture.

* Preheat oven to 350 degrees F. Bake for 2 to 2½ hours, until cabbage is red-brown and meat soft.

Serves 8.

---

1 The broth can be used later instead of water for your pilaf.

FISH

St. Nikolas Day Carp with Walnut Stuffing
Nikuldensky Sharan[1]

6-7-pound carp

2 teaspoons salt

10-12 ground black peppercorns

6 tablespoons olive oil

1 red onion, finely chopped

¾ cup crushed walnuts

¼ cup bread crumbs

1 white onion, finely chopped

2 tablespoons tomato paste

2 tablespoons flour

2-3 allspice seeds, ground

1 cup white wine

1-2 bay leaves

* Disembowel the carp, scrape off big scales if any, wash, dry with a paper towel, and sprinkle with salt and black pepper.

* In a saucepan lightly simmer 2 tablespoons olive oil, 1 tablespoon water, the red onion, walnuts, and crumbs.

* Fill the abdomen of the carp with stuffing, and sew well with a big needle. Grease a baking pan with olive oil and place the carp inside. Pour ½ cup boiling water over the carp and bake in a 350 degree oven for an hour or so.

For the sauce:

* Put the remaining 4 tablespoons olive oil in a saucepan, add 3 tablespoons of water, and the white onion and

---

1 A traditional dish for the dinner celebrating the Eastern Orthodox Saint Nikola, believed to be the guardian of fishermen and their catch.

simmer until the onions turn glossy. Add the tomato paste after mixing it in a spoon of hot water. Mix the flour in 2 tablespoons of warm water. Add the black pepper, allspice, wine, and the bay leaves. Lightly simmer until the liquid evaporates and only oil remains.

*Pour the sauce over the carp and bake in the oven for another 2 to 3 minutes.

Serves 6.

Sea Bass in White Wine
Lavrak S Byalo Vino

1 onion
1 tablespoon butter
8 sea bass fillets
1 teaspoon salt
½ cup white wine
8 ounces whipping cream

*Mince the onion. Put in a saucepan with melted butter, add fillets, and saute until light brown 3 to 4 minutes on each side.

*Add salt and white wine, cover, and cook for 5 minutes on low heat.

*Place the fillets very carefully on a serving plate. Boil down sauce in which fish was cooked. Remove from heat and add whipping cream.

*Mix and add over the fillets. Serve while hot.

Serves 4.

Mackerel in Lemon Sauce
Skumriya S Limon

3-3½ pounds of mackerel
2 teaspoons salt
16 tablespoons butter
1-2 carrots, diced
1 onion, diced
1 celery root, diced
4 tomatoes, diced
2 teaspoons crushed black peppercorns
2 bay leaves
½ cup chopped parsley
1 lemon

* Clean, rinse, and salt fish with 1 teaspoon salt. Place in a baking dish.

* Dice carrot, onion, and celery root. Melt butter in saucepan, add carrots, onion, celery root, tomatoes, remaining 1 teaspoon salt, pepper, and bay leaves. Cook on medium heat until the vegetables are cooked, 20 to 30 minutes.

* Pour content of saucepan over the fish. Chop parsley. Cut lemon in thin circles. Sprinkle parsley over fish and decorate each fish with a lemon slice.

* Preheat oven to 350 degrees F. Bake for 40 minutes.

Serves 6.

Turbot with Tomato Sauce
Gotven Kalkan

For the fish:
   8 slices turbot
   1½ teaspoons salt
   2 tablespoons flour
   ¼ cup oil

For the sauce:
   4 tomatoes
   1 onion
   2 tablespoons oil
   16 pitted olives, cut in fourths
   1 tablespoon butter
   1 teaspoon salt
   ½ cup chopped fresh parsley
   10 small anchovies

*Wash and dry the fish. Salt and flour the slices. Fry them in oil on both sides until brown (6 to 7 minutes). Place on a serving platter.

For the sauce:

*Peel and chop the tomatoes.

*Mince onion. Heat oil in saucepan, and brown onion for 3 minutes. Add tomatoes and cook until juice evaporates (6 to 7 minutes).

*In a frying pan, sauté the olives, salt and parsley in the butter for 1 minute. Pour the olive mixture together into the saucepan with the onions and tomatoes.

*Pour the hot sauce over the fish and place one anchovy on each slice.

Serves 4.

Fillets of Sole with Tartar Sauce
Pisiya Sus Sos Tartar

1 lemon
1 teaspoon salt
½ cup flour
4 eggs
½ cup bread crumbs
16 sole fillets
½ cup oil

For the sauce:
  ½ cup oil
  1 egg yolk
  1 teaspoon mustard
  1 teaspoon capers
  10 gherkins, chopped
  ½ cup chopped fresh parsley

*Put in 4 dishes in front of you: 1. Juice squeezed from lemon mixed with salt; 2. Flour; 3. Beaten eggs; 4. Bread crumbs

*Coat each filet with contents of each dish, in order, and fry in oil on both sides until brown.

*Place in a warm serving dish.

For the sauce:

*Make a mayonnaise by beating the oil, egg yolk, and mustard together.

*Add capers, gherkins, and parsley. Cover filets with sauce.

Serves 4 to 6.

Red Mullet with Dill Sauce
Barbuna S Domati

8 red mullets
1 lemon
4 tomatoes
1 onion
1 tablespoon butter
1 green pepper
2 bay leaves
2 teaspoons salt
¼ cup chopped fresh dill
16 pitted olives, cut in four

* Clean, wash, and dry the fish. Place in a buttered baking dish.

* Peel lemon and cut into fine slices, removing the seeds. Peel, seed and dice tomatoes.

* Chop onion. Heat butter in a saucepan and saute onion until glossy. Slice pepper into shreds and add to onions with tomatoes, bay leaves, and salt. Cook for 5 minutes.

* Put chopped dill, olives, and lemon slices over the fish, and pour the sauce over all.

* Preheat oven to 350 degrees F. Cover dish and bake in oven for 10 minutes.

Serves 2 to 4.

Gray Mullet with Carrots and Potatoes
Kefal S Cartofy I Morkovy

2 onions
8 cloves garlic
¼ cup olive oil
4 potatoes
4 carrots
2 tomatoes
1 teaspoon salt
2½ pounds of gray mullet
1½ lemons
1¼ cup chopped fresh parsley

*Mince onions and garlic. Warm 2 tablespoons oil in a saucepan and brown onions and garlic. Add ½ to ¾ cup water and cook for 5 to 6 minutes. Press through strainer with a wooden spoon.

*Cut potatoes into 1- x 2-inch pieces. Cut carrots crosswise into ½-inch circles. Peel and then dice tomatoes. Place vegetables together with onion purée in large pan. Add salt. Cook until vegetables are tender, about 25 minutes.

*Cut each gray mullet crosswise into 2 long pieces. Add to vegetables, cover, and cook for another 20 minutes.

*Remove pan from heat. Squeeze ½ lemon on top and leave to cool. Garnish with slices of remaining lemon and chopped parsley.

Serves 4.

Baked Mussels
Pecheny Midy

16 large mussels with shells
8 tablespoons butter
5 cloves garlic, chopped
juice of 1½ lemons
½ teaspoon salt
1 teaspoon crushed black peppercorns

* Open mussels and remove from shells. Wash 4 shells very well and put aside. Clean, wash and dry the mussels.

* Place 4 mussels in each shell. Place shells on a baking dish.

* Melt butter in saucepan, add garlic, lemon juice, salt, and pepper. Mix and pour over shells.

* Preheat oven to 350 degrees F. Bake for 5 to 6 minutes.

Serves 4.

GAME

The forests and mountains of Bulgaria have been famous for their game since ancient times. There are many historical records describing hunting expeditions in those parts, menus of hunter's feasts, types of game, and so on throughout the last millennium and a half.

Arab geographers have recorded some details about the trips of the sporting Ottoman sultan, Mehmed Avci the Hunter. Some 300 years ago he organized expeditions from Edirne to the eastern Balkan mountain range where he hunted bear, deer, wild boar, and wild cat.

More than a thousand years before him, again from the southern parts of the Peninsula, the Macedonian King Philip led an expedition during which he conquered the tallest peak at the center of the Balkan range. The eyewitness description of this expedition contains information about wild goat hunting and the preparation of game meals.

A couple of centuries after Philip's hunting exploits, the greatest among emperors who visited the Bulgarian mountains and feasted on their game, climbed the western slopes of the Balkan range. That was emperor Trajan who came here all the way from Rome to inspect the completion of his great road construction project from the Mediterranean sea to Dacia and the Danube. A triumph arch was built at a pass between Constantinople and Serdica, which stood until a century ago, to celebrate his arrival at the point where the East-West road through the peninsula crossed the north-south main road from Tessalonikae on the Aegean Sea to Riciaria on the Danube. Gorgeous camp tents were set, and many days of hunting game, picking wild berries, and gathering mushrooms took place. Needless to say a lot of cooking went on. Trajan was known for his love of winged game garnished with mushrooms. His favorite was a chestnut-flavored, red-topped, yellow-bottomed variation of the Amanita fungus family, which had almost disappeared from the Italian peninsula but was still in abundance here. We have no idea whether this meal was close to the very old traditional Duck with Mushrooms (See *Poultry* chapter, page 129). We do know, though, that it was at this feast that the rare red-yellow mushroom that went with fowl was named *Amanita Cesarae* in honor of Emperor Trajan.

We only regret that there is no room in this book to say more about the sixty-odd kinds of wild mushrooms that have been traditionally picked in Bulgaria and cooked with game.

Rabbit with Seed Onions
Popska Yahniya (Chumlek) Ot Zayak

For the marinade:
- 2-pound rabbit
- 1 celery root
- 2 bay leaves
- 1 cup white wine, or wine vinegar

For the yahniya:
- ¼ cup oil
- 2 medium onions
- 2 tablespoons tomato paste
- 1 tablespoon flour
- 1 teaspoon paprika
- ½ teaspoon crushed black pepper
- 2 bay leaves
- ¼ cup white wine
- 1 teaspoon salt
- 1 pound seed onions
- 10 cloves garlic, crushed
- 2 tomatoes, diced
- ½ lemon, sliced into fine circles

* Clean the rabbit, wash thoroughly, and cut into pieces. Cut celery root in two. Put bay leaves, celery, and meat into wine. Let meat stay in marinade for 6 to 10 hours.

* Take out rabbit meat and wash.

* Heat 2 tablespoons oil in a saucepan. Sauté meat for 5 to 6 minutes and remove meat from pan.

* Chop the medium onions. Sauté in the same oil as the meat for 2 to 3 minutes. Add tomato paste, flour (mixing it in), paprika, pepper, bay leaves, 2 tablespoons wine, 1 cup water, and salt.

* Bring sauce to boil, add meat, and simmer on low heat 10 to 12 minutes.

* In a separate saucepan, sauté onions in 2 tablespoons oil. Add garlic, tomatoes, lemon, and the rest of wine.

* Mix together the content of the two saucepans. Simmer at low heat until most of the liquid is evaporated.

Serves 4 to 6.

Deer Stew
Zadushena Surna

For the marinade:
   3 pounds deer meat
   2 cups white wine, or wine vinegar
   1 celery root, cut in two
   2 bay leaves

For the deer stew:
   ¼ cup oil
   4 onions
   1 carrot, diced
   1 celery root
   1 tablespoon tomato paste
   1 tablespoon flour
   1 teaspoon paprika
   ½ cup white wine
   2-3 bay leaves
   1 teaspoon crushed black pepper
   1 teaspoon salt
   4 potatoes, diced

* Clean the deer meat and wash thoroughly. Place in non-metallic container with wine or vinegar, celery root, and bay leaves. Marinate in refrigerator for 48 hours.
* Take meat out of marinade and cut into 1- x 1-inch pieces.
* Heat 2 tablespoons oil in a saucepan and sauté meat pieces for 4 to 5 minutes. Remove meat from pan.
* In same oil, sauté 3 chopped onions, carrot, and celery root, 1 whole onion, flour mixed with tomato paste, and paprika. Add wine, bay leaves, black pepper, and salt. Simmer for another 3 minutes.
* Add 1 cup hot water. Add meat, cover, and sauté on low heat for 15 minutes, until meat is almost perfectly soft.
* Add potatoes. Let simmer until meat is done (another 20 minutes). Take out meat for the second time and mash vegetables in the sauce.
* Serve meat in a serving dish with vegetable mixture.
* Garnish to taste.[1]

Serves 4 to 6.

---

1 Suggested garnish: Rice Pilaf (page 82), or Steamed Potatoes with Butter (page 66).

Baked Partridges
Pecheny Pudpudutsi[1]

For the partridges:

2-3 pounds partridges

1 teaspoon salt

1 teaspoon paprika

1 pound bacon

1 tablespoon butter, melted

For the sauce:

1 tablespoon flour

½ cup white wine

1 teaspoon crushed black pepper

½ teaspoon salt

* Clean partridges; discard heads and legs. Wash well.

* Cover with salt and paprika.

* Cut bacon in very thin strips, as long as possible. Wrap partridges in bacon strips, and tie with string.

* Arrange in a baking pan. Pour butter on top, and add ¼ cup hot water. Preheat oven to 350 degrees.

* Bake partridges 30 to 45 minutes, turning every 15 minutes. Put partridges aside.

* Prepare sauce in the remaining fat. Sauté flour, stirring well. Add wine, black pepper, and salt, and a little water, if necessary. Simmer for 5 to 6 minutes.

* Cut partridges in half along the spine bone, place in serving dish, and pour sauce on top of them. Garnish.[2]

Serves 6.

---

1   Quails, and doves could be prepared the same way.

2   Suggested garnishing: Rice Pilaf (page 82), Steamed Potatoes with Butter (page 66), or French Fries.

Wild Goose Stew[1]
Zadushena Diva Guska

For the marinade:
  1 wild goose
  2 cups white wine, or wine vinegar
  1 celery root
  2 bay leaves

For the goose stew:
  ¼ cup oil
  3 onions, diced
  2 garlic cloves, diced
  2 carrots
  ½ celery root
  1 tablespoon tomato paste
  1 tablespoon flour
  ¾ cup white wine
  2 bay leaves
  1 teaspoon crushed black pepper
  1 teaspoon salt
  1 teaspoon paprika, optional

* Clean the goose meat and wash thoroughly. Put in wine. Add celery root cut in two, and bay leaves. Let meat stay in marinade for 48 hours in refrigerator.

* Take meat out of marinade and cut into pieces.

* In a saucepan heat oil. Sauté meat, until red on all sides, without allowing to dry (4 to 5 minutes).

* Take meat out. In same oil sauté onions, garlic, carrots, and celery root for 4 to 5 minutes, until soft. Add tomato paste and flour. Mix well, add 2 tablespoons hot water,

---

1 A wild duck could be prepared the same way.

and mix. Add wine, bay leaves and black pepper. Add paprika if desired.

*Salt meat and put back in saucepan. Tightly cover saucepan and simmer on low heat for 35 to 40 minutes, until meat is soft.

*Garnish to taste.[1]

Serves 4.

Pheasant Stew[2]
Zadushen Fazan

For the marinade:
   2 wild pheasants
   2 cups white wine, or wine vinegar
   1 celery root, or 2 celery stalks
   2 bay leaves

For the pheasant stew:
   ¼ pound bacon
   6 tablespoons butter
   ½ cup very small onions
   3 carrots, diced
   1 tablespoon flour
   1 tablespoon tomato paste
   ½ cup white wine
   2 tablespoons cognac
   1 teaspoon crushed black pepper

---

1   Suggested garnish: Rice Pilaf (page 82), Steamed Potatoes with Butter (page 66)

2   A wood-grouse could be prepared the same way.

¼ cup chopped fresh parsley
½ cup milk or whipping cream

* The birds have to stay in the refrigerator for two days before plucking.
* Pluck and disembowel, and leave in refrigerator for one more night.
* Clean, wash, and cut into portions. Put in an enamel container and add wine, celery root, and bay leaves. Let stay in marinade for 8 to 9 hours.
* Drain pheasant pieces. Cut bacon into fine strips. Sauté bacon and pheasant in a saucepan in butter for 6 to 7 minutes, until red.
* Remove pheasant from butter.
* In same saucepan, sauté small onions, carrots, flour (which should be mixed well), and tomato paste, until onions and carrots are soft, 8 to 10 minutes.
* Add ½ cup hot water, wine, and cognac. After sauce is brought to boil, add meat. Add black pepper and parsley. Cover well and simmer until meat is soft, 35 to 40 minutes.
* Place meat on a serving dish.
* Strain sauce, stir with a wooden spoon, and add whipping cream. Mix and pour over meat.
* Garnish to taste.[1]

Serves 4 to 6.

---

1 Suggested garnish: Steamed Potatoes with Butter (page 66)

Doves with Peas
Guluby S Grah

6 doves

3 onions

¼ pound bacon

8 tablespoons butter

1½ pounds fresh peas

1 teaspoon salt

1 tablespoon flour

* Pluck and disembowel the doves. Wash well. Cut off and discard legs and heads.

* Dice onions and bacon. Put into a pot together with butter, doves, and ¼ cup water. Cover well, turn up heat, and simmer for 30 minutes.

* Add 1½ cups water, peas, and salt. Simmer for another 30 minutes.

* Move doves to a serving plate.

* Put flour in a separate bowl. Slowly add sauce from boiling peas into bowl, stirring vigorously, until flour mixture is perfectly smooth. Add flour back into pot with peas. Stir, and simmer for another 10 to 15 minutes.

Serves 4 to 6.

BREADS AND PASTRIES

*B*reads and pastries have one thing in common: both are produced by mixing flour with liquids into a dough, which is then kneaded into different shapes and forms.

The basic difference between breads and pastries is that breads are prepared with different agents that are added to the dough not only to make the dough rise, but to give the final product a specific flavor. The Bulgarian baking tradition is pre-medieval, and still involves the use of many different rising agents for breads. There are four basic ones:

—Sour dough (which is a 5000-year-old agent)

—Chick-pea yeast (which gives the finest flavor to pastries)[1]

—Hop vine yeast (which is used for dry breads and long-lasting biscuits)

—Bread yeast (which is applied in a number of ways depending on which culinary effect one is trying to achieve).[2]

The second difference between breads and pastries is that pastry dough is divided into small pieces, which are then rolled out into thin dough leaves with a rolling pin, or pulled by hand.

The following section of this cookbook will give the principle method of producing dough and fillo leaves. Specific differences will be pointed out where necessary.

---

1   Other yeasts are used with special pastries, like sesame-yeast for certain types of milinky.

2   Baking soda, another rising agent for flour products, is unknown in old Bulgarian traditional cooking.

Basic Dough

2 cups flour

1 egg

dash of salt

* Sift the flour. Set aside 2 to 3 tablespoons.

* Pour the flour into a large bowl. In hollow in the middle, put egg, dash of salt, and ¼ cup water. Mix.

* Spread some flour on tabletop. Take dough out and knead with the palm of your hand, turning the end of the dough in. If the dough sticks to the table or your hands while kneading, sprinkle some of the set aside flour on the table. Knead again and again until no more bubbles are seen in the dough, and until you feel the dough pushing back against the bottom of your palm when you push in to knead.

* Put dough back into the bowl, sprinkle some flour over it and cover with a damp cloth. Let sit for 20 minutes.

Fillo Leaves Preparation

* Divide dough into 12 pieces and roll them into balls.

* Cover them with a damp cloth and let them sit for another 30 minutes.

* With a rolling pin, roll out 3 balls to a thickness of 1½ inches (disks approximately 3 inches in diameter). Spread melted butter on top of each disk. Put one on top of the other and roll out to obtain the fillo leaf—a very thin disk approximately 18 inches in diameter. If the dough sticks, sprinkle more flour on the table.

Repeat process to make four 18-inch disks.

Sliven Butter Cakes with Chick-Pea Yeast

Sivensky Milinky

20 dry chick-pea grains

3 cups flour

1 tablespoon salt

6 tablespoons oil

6 tablespoons fat

16 tablespoons butter, melted

1 egg

5 tablespoons powdered sugar

For the chick-pea yeast:

* Crush chick-pea grains. Rub between fingers to discard shells.
* Put in a bottle and pour boiling water over them. Pour warm water out immediately for the chick-pea bulgur to start swelling. Pour in boiling water again. Add pinch of salt. Let stay for 10 to 12 hours at 67 to 73 degrees F.

For the milinky:

* Mix 2 cups flour, yeast, and 2 cups cold water. Cover and set in a warm place (69 degrees F) for 60 minutes until it rises. Knead again.
* Prepare the milinky with hands, dipping your fingers from time to time in the oil and the fat. The milinky cakes should be rolled into small balls, ¾ inch in diameter at the most. Place tightly, one next to the other in a medium baking pan.
* Cover pan and let dough rise for another 1 hour in a warm place.

* Mix the remaining 1 cup flour, with ½ cup water, and the melted butter. Pour over the milinky cakes in the pan.
* After the rising is completed and the topping is partially absorbed, use a brush to spread over the beaten egg.
* Preheat oven to 350 degrees F. Bake until the milinky are red-brown on top, and the edges along the rim of the pan are lightly burnt (30 to 40 minutes).
* Sprinkle with powdered sugar. Serve warm.

Serves 4 to 6.

Feta Cheese Pie
Tutmanik

4 eggs
½ cup yogurt
½ teaspoon baking soda
16 tablespoons (2 sticks) butter
½ pound feta cheese
1 pound (3 cups) flour

* Reserve 1 egg yolk. Beat the remaining eggs and white in a big bowl. Add yogurt, baking soda, 15 tablespoons melted butter, cheese, and flour. Mix into a medium-firm dough.
* Grease a 9- x 2- inches baking pan with remaining butter. Spread in the dough.
* Beat last yolk and brush over dough.
* Preheat oven to 350 degrees F. Bake until red-brown, about 35 to 45 minutes.

Serves 8.

Sesame Bagels
Gevretsy

1 tablespoon yeast
2 pounds (5½ cups) flour
1 teaspoon salt
2 tablespoons sesame seeds
8 tablespoons sugar

* Dissolve yeast in 1 cup water.
* In a big salad bowl, mix flour, water with yeast, and salt.
* Cover and leave for 30 minutes in a warm room, or low heat oven, to rise.
* Knead dough. Tear apart into 8 to 10 pieces. Roll each piece about 1 finger thick and 2 feet long. Form into a circle with a diameter of 3 to 4 inches.
* Sprinkle flour over bottom of baking pan. Arrange bagels at least ½ inch apart. Cover and put in low heat oven for 10 to 15 minutes to rise some more.
* Mix 6 cups warm water with sugar. Bring water to boil. Drop bagels in warm water and boil for 3 to 4 minutes.
* Take out and arrange on cookie sheet. Cover with sesame seed.
* Preheat oven to 350 degrees F. Bake until red-brown, 30 to 35 minutes.

Yields 8 to 10 bagels.

Cheese Pastry
Banitsa[1]

1 cup flour

3 eggs

1 dash salt

2 tablespoons water

½ pound feta cheese

2 tablespoons milk or yogurt, optional

1 dash caraway seed, optional

8 tablespoons butter, melted

* Sift ¾ cup flour and make a hollow in the middle. Put in 1 egg, the salt and the water. Mix and knead. If while kneading the dough sticks to the table or your hands, sprinkle some flour on the table. Divide into 12 pieces and roll them into balls. Flatten each piece, and cover them with a damp cloth for 30 minutes.

* Mash the feta cheese. Mix 2 whole eggs in a bowl with the milk, a dash of caraway seed (optional), and the cheese.

* Roll out the dough leaves as for fillo (See page 156). Place a rolled out fillo leaf into a 12- x 2-inch buttered pan, with the edges of dough coming slightly over the edges of the pan.

* Roll out another group of 3 dough balls the same way, butter the ones in the pan, and place the new triple layer on top.

* When you have only 6 dough balls left, spread the cheese and egg filling in the pan.

---

1   The banitsa is a central part at the traditional Bulgarian New Year's dinner. *Kusmeti* (fortunes) are placed in it for each member of the family. The banitsa is turned around like a roulette, and everyone can find out from his slice what to expect during the New Year: love, wisdom, money, good health, etc.

*Repeat the process with two more fillo layers. Butter before putting a new fillo leaf in the baking pan. Cut out the "skirts" of the fillo leaves that are hanging out of the baking pan.[1] Butter the top liberally, distributing with the spreading brush whatever is left of the melted butter along the edges of the pan.

*Preheat the oven to 350 degrees for 25 to 35 minutes, until the top of the banitsa is golden brown.

Serves 6 to 8.

Cheese Pastry with Ready-Made Fillo Leaves[2]
Banitsa S Gotovy Listy

1 pound fillo leaves

½ pound feta cheese

3 eggs

2 tablespoons soda water

8 tablespoons butter, melted

1 dash of salt

2 tablespoons sour milk or yogurt, optional

1 dash caraway seed, optional

*This variation of the banitsa is prepared the same way as Banitsa in the previous recipe by spreading the fillo leaves out of the edges of the baking pan and buttering

---

1   The traditional banitsa baking pan is copper and its sharp edges are facing up in a way which helps cut off the excess fillo leafs by just pressing with one's open palm over the edge.

2   This is the more popular ("lazy") way of preparing the banitsa. It saves the time consuming preparation of the banitsa leaves which, to a great extent, deprives the consumer of the palatable effect of this Bulgarian classic.

them in between with the melted butter. Half the fillo leaves should be layered on the bottom of pan, then the cheese filling, followed by the remaining leaves. The only difference is that the filling should contain some yogurt instead of milk, and that here and there among the fillo leaves after buttering them, some soda water should be sprinkled, no matter how lightly.[1]

Rolled Cheese Pastry
Vita Banitsa

* Use the same ingredients as in Banitsa (page 160).

* Prepare fillo leaves the same way as the leaves in Banitsa.[2]

* Spread out one fillo leaf and cut along the diameter, producing 2 half circles. Starting from the center of the straight side, cut each half into four 4 triangles.

* Place a tablespoon of cheese filling at the base of each triangle. Roll towards the point, folding in the 2 sides to

---

1 The reason for this is that the commercial fillo leaf is very dry and contains preservatives which "kill" the potential of the dough to absorb, mix, and rise even without soda or yeast-enhancing stimulants. The traditional home-prepared banitsa leaves slightly rise before the baking is over. The butter and part of the cheese fat and the egg are absorbed by them, which makes them fluffy, fragrant, and impossible to stop eating. The commercial-leaf banitsa doesn't absorb either the taste of its filling, or the butter. This makes it relatively dry, less tasty, and greasy. And this, of course, makes all the difference in the world! Play with the dough, learn how to knead, sprinkle flour on your dough ball, press it in with the bottom of your palm and feel it rising against your hand and kicking back, and then you will know what the art of cooking is all about! Become human again!

2 Store-bought fillo dough can be used with the same effect as when it is used for the *banitsa* (page 160).

prevent the filling from leaking out. Every time you roll a triangle over, spread melted butter on the upper side of the roll with a brush. Roll buttered part in and butter the new side. The final result will produce 32 cigar shaped cheese pastries about 1 inch thick and 5 to 6 inches long.

* Arrange rolls in a baking pan. Butter on top and bake as described in the banitsa recipe.

Serves 8 to 10.

Milk Fillo Dough Pastry
Mlechna Banitsa

8 tablespoons butter
1 pound fillo dough[1]
5 eggs
1½ quarts (6 cups) milk
1½ cups sugar
1 dash (6 drops) of vanilla extract
Option 1: **12 teaspoons powdered sugar**
Option 2: **1 egg yolk and 3 tablespoons sugar**

* Melt the butter.

* Very lightly grease a 12- x 15- x 2-inch baking pan. Spread the fillo leaves in the pan, one by one. If pan is smaller fold them so that they are slightly larger than the bottom of the pan. While doing this butter them in between with the melted butter.

* Cut the *banitsa* into 12 slices (dividing the banitsa into 3 strips lengthwise, and then each strip into 4). Preheat

---

1 Store-bought fillo dough can be used with the same effect as when it is used for the *banitsa* (page 160).

oven to 350 degrees F. Bake for 30 to 35 minutes, until the top of the banitsa starts turning brown. Take out of oven.

* Beat the eggs in a 3-quart bowl, then add the milk, sugar, and vanilla and stir until well mixed. This could be done while the baking is taking place. (For Option 2 set aside 1 cup of the mix.) Pour the mix on top of the *banitsa.*

* Bake for another 35 to 45 minutes, until the top of the banitsa turns pleasantly red.

* *Option 1:* Lightly sprinkle powdered sugar on top of each slice.

* *Option 2:* To the 1 cup of the mix, add the egg yolk and sugar, beat into thick cream, and pour over each slice when serving.

Serves 12.

Walnut and Sugar Syrup Pastry
Baklava

2 eggs
½ cup flour
1½ cups sugar
1 teaspoon cinnamon
1½ lemon
½ cup crushed walnuts
1 pound fillo leaves
8 tablespoons butter, melted
½ teaspoon vanilla

For the filling:

* Beat eggs. Add flour, ½ cup sugar, cinnamon, juice from half lemon and its grated skin, and crushed walnuts. Mix.

For the baklava:

* Arrange half of the fillo leaves in a 9- x 11- x 2-inch baking pan, folding in the excess parts of the leaves to fit in the pan. Brush melted butter between layers of fillo leaves.
* When half of the leaves are done, spread walnut filling over them.
* Cover with the rest of the leaves, brushing melted butter between them.
* Cut baklava into 16 or 24 square pieces (4 rows of 4, or 4 rows of 6). Butter the top liberally, distributing with the spreading brush whatever is left of the melted butter along the edges of the pan.
* Preheat oven to 350 degrees F and bake for 25 to 35 minutes, until the top of the baklava in golden brown.

For the syrup:

* Put remaining 1 cup sugar into 1½ cups water, adding the vanilla, and the rest of the lemon and grated lemon skin.
* Boil on low heat, stirring from time to time, until syrup thickens enough, so that a drop of it runs with difficulty down a tilted dish.
* Pour half of syrup on baklava while both are hot. Cover with a cloth or paper. Let baklava sit overnight.
* Pour rest of syrup over baklava and let stay for at least 4-6 hours, until syrup is absorbed by the fillo.

Serves 16 to 24.

Leek Pastry
Prasena Banitsa

3 eggs
½ pound feta cheese
1½ pounds leeks, chopped
⅛ cup sour milk or yogurt
2 tablespoons soda water
1 pound fillo leaves[1]
8 tablespoons butter, melted

For the filling:

* Beat eggs. Add crushed cheese, chopped leeks, sour milk or yogurt, and soda water. Mix.

For the banitsa:

* Arrange half of the fillo leaves in a rectangular baking pan, folding in the excess parts of the leaves to fit in the pan. Brush melted butter between layers of fillo leaves.

* When half of the leaves are done spread the leek filling over them.

* Cover with the rest of the leaves, brushing melted butter between them.

* Cut pastry into 16 square pieces. Butter the top, liberally distributing with the spreading brush whatever is left of the melted butter along the edges of the pan.

* Preheat oven to 350 degrees F and bake for 40 to 50 minutes, until the top of the banitsa is golden brown.

Serves 16.

---

1 Store-bought fillo dough can be used with the same effect as when it is used for the *banitsa* (page 160).

Pumpkin Pastry
Tikvenik

2 eggs
½ cup crushed walnuts
1½ pounds fresh pumpkin, grated
¼ cup sugar
1 dash of salt
½ teaspoon cinnamon
2 tablespoons soda water
1 pound fillo leaves[1]
10 tablespoons butter, melted

For the filling:

* Beat eggs. Add walnuts, pumpkin, sugar, salt, cinnamon, and soda water. Mix.

For the pastry:

* Arrange half of the fillo leaves in a 9- x 11- x 2-inch baking pan folding in the excess parts of the leaves to fit in the pan, and brushing melted butter on each fillo leaf.

* When half of the leaves are done, spread the pumpkin filling on them.

* Cover with the rest of the leaves, brushing melted butter between them.

* Cut pastry into 16 square pieces. Butter the top, liberally distributing with the spreading brush whatever is left of the melted butter along the edges of the pan.

* Preheat oven to 350 degrees F and bake for 35 to 40 minutes, until the top of the banitsa is golden brown.

Serves 16.

---

1   Store-bought fillo dough can be used with the same effect as when it is used for the *banitsa* (page 160).

DESSERTS

*S*weets were not part of the classical Bulgarian menu. Their consumption used to have more or less a ritualistic character and often was directly part of a religious tradition. The *kozoonatsy* at Easter breakfast and the *banitsa*, or the *kolachy* on the night before Christmas, were generally looked upon as the symbol of hospitality in a Bulgarian home, as a token of giving.

Originally this came from the old Bulgarian traditional dinner. The family would gather around the short legged round dinner table (the *sofra*) on the floor. The father then would say the prayer asking God to come and eat with them, and would break the bread, handing a piece to everyone. When dinner was over, if it was a holiday, the keeper of the house, the mother, acted out God's giving to the family (*Blago-dad* : the Giving of God's Sweetness). Breaking the fast with sweets was called "*o-blag-vam se*," or "o-blaj-vam-se" ("getting the sweet"), getting God's good-giving. Sweets were something special, something out of the ordinary, ususally something fruity, sugary, or full of honey.

Even today common Bulgarians believe in the back of their minds that sweets are for guests; the coming of guests, of course, being the coming of the big and sacred "Outside" into the house. And the housewife is obligated to perform the Good-giving of the Universal Spirit in the home where her children are raised to love and obey the rules.

Visitors from the West are perplexed by the hysterical insistence of Bulgarian housewives that they break their own sacred Western diets the moment they cross the threshold of Bulgarian homes. Don't reject their innocent sootlash or butter cookie. It is like telling the mother of that household that she has been denied the sacred privilege of being the agent of God's good giving.

Rice Puding
Sootlash

1 cup rice
8 cups milk
½ cup cornstarch
1½ cups powdered sugar
Cinnamon (as needed)

* Cover and cook the rice at low heat in 1½ cups of water, until water evaporates, about 15 to 25 minutes.

* Put the milk and cooked rice in a saucepan, boil, and then reduce heat to simmer.

* Put the cornstarch in a bowl. Slowly add ¾ cup of water, stirring constantly, to make a smooth paste. Add it slowly to the simmering milk, stirring constantly. Cook for 10 minutes still stirring.

* Add the sugar and cook until it thickens, never ceasing to stir.

* Divide into individual bowls and cool. Sprinkle with cinnamon.

Serves 8 to 10.

Rice Flour-Milk Cream
Maleby

4 cups milk
1 cup sugar
¾ cups rice flour
2 tablespoons rose water
½ cup preferred fruit syrup, optional

* Boil the milk with the sugar.
* Dissolve rice flour in 2 to 3 tablespoons cold water. Add to milk and stir without stopping for 5 to 6 minutes.
* Pour into 4 to 6 dessert bowls, and cool.
* If you desire, pour equal amounts of syrup on top of dessert bowls.

Serves 4 to 6.

Shredded Pastry with Walnuts
Kadaif

16 tablespoons (2 sticks) butter
2 pounds kadaif (shredded phillo dough)
1 cup crushed or ground walnuts
3 pounds (6¾ cups) sugar
Juice of 1 lemon
1 teaspoon cinnamon

* Melt 8 tablespoons butter in a 9- x 11- x 3-inch cake pan.
* Spread half of the kadaif on the bottom of the pan. Spread the walnuts over the kadaif. Spread the rest of the kadaif over the walnuts.

* Cut remaining 8 tablespoons butter into small pieces and put on top of the kadaif.
* Preheat oven to 300 degrees F. (While kadaif is baking, prepare syrup.) Bake until top of kadaif turns golden brown, 20 to 25 minutes.

For the syrup:

* Put sugar to boil in 2½ cups water for 5 minutes.
* Add lemon juice and cinnamon.
* Pour over cooled kadaif.

Serves 12 to 15.

Semolina with Walnuts
Gris Halva

8 tablespoons butter

1 cup semolina

1 cup sugar

½ cup crushed walnuts

½ teaspoon cinnamon

* Melt butter in saucepan, add semolina, mix, and simmer until semolina turns golden brown (10 to 15 minutes).
* Boil sugar in 1½ cups water for 5 minutes. Pour syrup over semolina, and stir until mixture starts boiling.
* Simmer for 3 minutes.
* Take off heat. Cover with a thick towel, put lid on top of towel for 15 to 20 minutes.
* Stir with a fork, and cover again.
* When mixture cools, mix crushed walnuts with cinnamon and sprinkle over semolina mixture.

Serves 6 to 8.

Butter Cookies
Masleny Koorabiy [1]

1 pound butter[2]
¾ pound sugar
2 pounds flour (7 cups)
½ teaspoon salt
30 whole cloves

* Beat the butter with a wooden spoon until it becomes soft and creamy (do not melt). Add sugar, flour, and salt and mix thoroughly.

* Knead the butter-sugar dough, and form small balls (about the size of Ping-Pong ball). Stick a clove on top of each one.

* Flour a baking pan, and discard excess flour. Arrange cookie balls in pan at least ½-inch apart.

* Preheat oven to 325 degrees F. Bake until cookies only start turning light golden-yellowish on top (16 to 20 minutes). Although they will be quite soft, immediately take out of the oven without touching them. Let them cool.

Makes 30 cookies.

---

1 This looks so simple, and yet it is a real challenge! When you bring the cookie toward your mouth, the clove should hit your nose with its aroma, and tongue sensitivity bursts to life, and the mouth starts watering. When you bite, it should be the triumph of crunchiness; but the crunchier the cookie, the greater the chance it will fall apart in your teeth, and crumble down all over your lips, chin, and shirt. The problem is that if you achieve a good crunch by baking a little longer, or at a higher heat, you most certainly will open a cavity inside your cookie (a danger with delayed action!) that you discover after you bite. It is a matter of the right combination of mixing the butter, kneading the cookies (and how big should they be!), and temperature during the baking. What butter cookies are to the competitive chef, is what flying targets are to the competitive sharp shooter! Play with them and you will see!

2 Soft full-body organic butter from a farmer's market will give you the best results.

Walnut Honey Cookies
Orehovy Medenky

1¼ pounds (4 cups) flour
2 eggs
2 tablespoons honey
½ pound (1¼ cups) sugar
1 cup oil
1 teaspoon baking soda
½ cup walnut halves

*Spread flour evenly in a baking pan. Add eggs, honey, sugar, oil, and baking soda. Knead into a fairly hard dough.

*Form dough into small Ping-Pong-sized balls.

*Put a walnut half on top of each ball.

*Preheat oven to 350 degrees F. Bake untill cookies start hardening, yet before they really are hard, 15 to 20 minutes.

Makes 20 to 25 cookies.

FRUITS AND FRUIT DISHES

Pumpkin in Syrup
Varena Tikva

3 to 3½-pound pumpkin
1¾ to 2 cups sugar
1 cup crushed walnuts

* Seed and peel the pumpkin. Cut it into 1-inch slices.

* Arrange slices in a flat saucepan. Spread the sugar on top and pour 2 cups water over the slices. Cover and cook on low heat for about 1 hour, until the pumpkin slices are tender.

* Cool. Arrange the pumpkin slices in serving dish. Pour the syrup from the pan over them and sprinkle the crushed walnuts on top.

Serves 8 to 10.

Baked Pumpkin
Pechena Tikva

3½ to 4-pound pumpkin
¼ cup water
1 to 1½ cups crushed walnuts
1 cup honey, optional

* Seed pumpkin without peeling it. Cut into 4- x 4-inch slices.

* Pour the water in a flat pan and arrange slices in it. Preheat oven to 350 degrees F. Bake for about 1 hour, until the pumpkin slices are tender and the skin around their edges is slightly burnt.

*Cool a bit. Arrange the pumpkin slices in serving dish. Sprinkle the crushed walnuts on top. Serve with teaspoon for scooping the baked pumpkin off the skin.

*Optional: Pour 1 teaspoon honey on top of each slice immediately before serving.

Serves 10 to 12.

Dried Apricots with Almonds[1] and Cream
Susheny Kaisiyy S Bademy

1 pound dried apricots
½ cup fresh almond pits
1 pound (2½ cups) sugar
1 pound (2 cups) fresh cream

*Put apricots and almonds in water overnight. Drain them.

*Peel skins of almonds.

*Place apricots in a saucepan and cover with water. Boil for 15 minutes. Pour off half of the water, add the sugar,

---

1 This time the nut used is not the favored walnut. The culinary effect of this combination is that genetically the apricot tree and the almond tree are very close, and some almond pits (which contain tiny amounts of anti-sclerosis cyanide like almonds do) are used in Bulgarian pastries and appetizers, as the almonds themselves are sometimes used. Replacing the apricot pit with its cousin, the pit of the almond fruit, is close to the natural fruit-pit match of the apricot, and yet one step removed, which sharpens the awareness of this cyanide combination. When we speak of an "almond fruit," of course, we should be aware that it does not grow as much fiber as the apricot one, and is perceived commonly as only a very thick skin. Still, it is very well known in Bulgarian cooking, and is used during August, when the almond is not totally developed but is still green and juicy, in Bulgarian stews— with mutton, beef, game, etc.

and boil for another 20 minutes. Stir carefully with a wooden spoon, so as not to break the apricots.

* Put apricots on a serving dish on their backs, with the opening where the pit was on top. Put a teaspoon of cream in the center of each. Stick a peeled almond in the middle. Pour syrup from the saucepan over the apricots.

Serves 12.

Fig Jam
Smokinovo Sladko

100 green figs
1 tablespoon lemon juice
2 pounds (5 cups) sugar
10 whole cloves
½ teaspoon vanilla, optional

* Wash figs, and skin them carefully. Put on gloves to protect your hands from getting stained.
* Put figs in cooking pot with 4 cups water, lemon juice, and sugar.
* Let sit for 24 hours. Cook at medium heat, discarding the froth all the time. Stir every 15 minutes with a wooden spoon. Cook until a drop of the syrup on a tilted dish won't run down.
* Take jam off the heat. Add cloves, if desired—vanilla, and stir gently one last time.

Serves 30 to 40.

Baked Quinces
Pecheny Dyuly

4 pounds quinces
½ pound (1¼ cups) sugar

* Wash quinces under running water.
* Cut in two and clean out seeds and seed parts.
* Arrange in a baking pan, skin side down. Distribute sugar in cavities.
* Preheat oven to 300 degrees F. Bake until brim of half fruits starts turning dark brown, 20 to 30 minutes.

Serves 6 to 8.

Prune Compote
Compot Ot Siny Slivy

1 pound dry prunes
1 pound (2½ cups) sugar

* Wash prunes under running water. Let stay in cold water for 20 minutes.
* Wash thoroughly two more times.
* Boil in 3 quarts water for 30 minutes.
* Add sugar and boil for another 5 minutes.
* Take off heat and cool. Serve cold.

Serves 16 to 18.

SOFT DRINKS

*B*ulgarians love fruit and are known for producing drinks from almost any fruit or wild berry one could think of.

The oldest referral to this tradition is in the medieval memoir of the ambassador of Emperor Oton the First to Constantinople Luidprand—"In Legacio." In this eighth-century report, the diplomat of the Holy Empire describes the brother of the Bulgarian Emperor Boris, whose delegates at the time were receiving annual tribute from Byzance and were well known to Luidprand. Mighty as Boris was, his younger brother Veniamin, who was educated in Constantinople to be a bishop, had denied his Christian name, took the pagan name Boyan, and escaped into the Rila high mountain wilderness. There he took to the old Bulgarian shaman traditions, performing pagan rituals during which he was known to have transformed himself into a wolf, or any wild animal at his will, and where he cooked the heavenly old Bulgarian nectar from the berries of wild dogwood trees and cranberry shrubs.

Today Boyan's recipe for Bulgarian cranberry juice is lost, yet traditional Bulgarian soft drinks are many, and the most popular ones are worth mentioning.

Cold Yogurt Drink
Ayran

2 pounds whole milk yogurt
4 cups cold water

*Mix yogurt and water thoroughly (with a mixer). Keep in the refrigerator for at least 1 hour before drinking.
Serves 8.

Radomir Sweet and Sour Rye Yeast Drink
Radomirska Boza[1]

*Rye grain, sweetened with sugar, is boiled. Bread yeast is added to start the ripening of the drink. Its enzymes help it ferment up to a 0.5 % alcohol sweet-sour drink.

Sweet and Sour Cold Drink
Sherbet

¼ pound (½ cup) sugar
3 tablespoons apple vinegar or lemon juice

*Dissolve the sugar in 4 cups water mixing vigorously for 2 to 3 minutes.

---

1 This most popular traditional Bulgarian soft drink is produced only industrially. We mention it here only for your information.

* Add vinegar (or lemon juice) and stir.
* Refrigerate and serve with ice.

Serves 4 to 6.

Grape Juice
Grozdov Sok (Shira)

20 pounds very ripe grapes

* Wash grapes under running water thoroughly. Pick grapes and put in a big container. Press well and pour into another container.
* Let grape juice sit for 3 to 4 hours to settle. 3 tablespoons clean wood ashes can be mixed in as purifier.
* Drain juice (without dregs) through a cheesecloth.
* Let sit for another 3-4 hours and do the same.
* Pour juice into an enamel pot and heat in water bath at 200 to 225 degrees F for 20 minutes, discarding froth as often as possible.
* Pour juice in bottles and keep in refrigerator.

Serves 25 to 30.

Elder Blossom Juice
Sok Ot Buz

2 pounds elder blossom
3 pounds (7½ cups) sugar
3 tablespoons wine vinegar

* Wash elder blossoms well, and pour 5 quarts of water over them. Add sugar and vinegar.
* Let sit 4 to 5 days, stirring thoroughly in the morning and in the evening.
* Drain juice thoroughly through cheesecloth, pour into bottles, cork bottles, and serve cold at your leisure.

Makes 24 to 26 cups.

Linden Blossom Tea
Lipov Chay

2 tablespoons of aromatic (female) linden tree blossoms with leaves
¼ cup sugar, optional
1 lemon, optional

* Boil 4¼ cups water in teapot. Add blossoms, put lid on, and take off heat.
* Let sit for at least 5 to 6 minutes.
* Cut lemon into ¼-inch circles, then cut each in two.
* Pour into 4 to 6 teacups, leaving blossoms in teapot covered with water.[1]

---

1 Only the second time around does the linden blossom tea release its full aroma.

* Store in refrigerator for a second usage, and adding the same amount of water, and pouring the same amount of tea.
* Offer sugar and lemon to be added individually to taste.

Yields 6 to 12 teacups in 2 usages.

Turkish Coffee
Toorsko Kafe

2 teaspoons brown roasted[1] Arabic coffee beans
2 teaspoons sugar

*Grind cofee to the finest powder possible.

*Put 1 teaspoon coffee, 1 teaspoon sugar in two[2] 2-ounce copper *djezbe* (narrow neck, long handled, copper coffee pots).

*Pour 2-ounces water in each *djezbe*, and stir well.

---

1 It is worth explaining here that from the point of view of the classic Near Eastern art of cooking, the dark toasts of French, Austrian, and Italian coffees is a sure mark of West European ignorance. The divine aroma of the Ethiopian coffee (from which the art of coffee making started) is the result of the roasting of the coffee bean until its oil is forced to release its flavor, which occurs at the point when it turns brown. When it is overroasted to "dark," the dark color is the color of burnt oil. Most of the coffee bean aroma is lost. The deep, sharp, macho flavor West Europeans enjoy in dark roasts is the flavor of the coffee bean tar left after it had been exposed to higher heat than the oil can survive, and it is very bad for the walls of your stomach.

2 One coffee cup—one *djezbe*! That used to be the principle of classical Near Eastern coffee houses. And that is the only way to prevent the coffee aroma from escaping when the boiling starts. It is achieved by means of closing the narrow neck of the *djezbe* with the thick foam which serves as a cork. Present day Turkish restaurants of the Industrial Era prepare coffee for four in one *djezbe*. Not in four *djezbes* as the old tradition would have it. When the coffee is brought to boil the idolized foam is distributed into four cups, and then the coffee itself is poured in. The foam surfaces on top, and the customer's cup looks exactly like one served in a nineteenth century Golden Horn coffee house, the only difference being that before the foam surfaces to the top, the aroma, which should have been kept under it in the *djezbe*, is half gone. A modern age "wonder coffee" to match our "Wonderbread."

* Heat 1 inch deep pure sand[1] on a hot plate. Bury the 2 *djezbes* in the sand.

* When bubbles start appearing on the surface, be prepared to take coffees off. Gradually foam will start rising in the narrow neck of the *djezbes*. Take *djezbes* out of the sand at the last moment before foam boils over.

* If hot plate with sand is unavailable, put the *djezbes* to boil on a hot plate. When the foam covers the *djezbe* neck lift up by the handle before it boils over. Wait half a minute for the foam to settle, and put back on the plate, holding the handle in readiness, until the foam starts rushing up again. Repeat 3 times without allowing it to boil over. Let *djezbe* stand ½ minute and pour in coffee cups.

Serves 2.

---

1 Metal stove tops in old coffee houses in Bulgaria, Rumania, Macedonia, Montenegro, and Turkey used to have a two-inch brim to allow the space to be filled with sand. This was done to ensure equal heating of the copper *djezbe* on all sides and at all levels of the vessel. It prevents the boisterous upward circulation of the coffee if heated only from the bottom (which is the case with common hot plates), and the rapid evaporation of much of the coffee bean flavor. The thick foam in the neck of the *djezbe* prevents the escape of the aroma, and that is how coffee masters were judged: by the thickness of their coffee foam.

WINES AND LIQUORS

Archeological wine studies show that wine has been produced in the Caucasian region since 5000 B.C. As far as written records go, the epic of "Gilgamesh" shows that it was known in Iraq since 1800 B.C. Homer's "Illiad," though, is the first piece of literature which mentions quality wine which was produced on the territory of Bulgaria by the Tracians since at least 1000 B.C. Scattered historical information about wine producing and wine drinking in Bulgaria (as a state) date back to the early Middle Ages. The first laws against drinking wine and forceful destruction of vineyards were passed by Bulgaria's King Krum during the eighth century.

Since the beginning of this century, Bulgaria has developed a number of well established wine labels and started exporting wines with success, winning good international recognition. During the 1970s, the Bulgarian Cabernet was very popular in Great Britain, Scandinavia, and Germany.

After Word War II, Bulgaria's wine export was gradually reoriented toward the Soviet Union. At its peak, Bulgaria exported more than 25 million cases of wine across the Black sea to Russia. This dependence on the Soviet market proved quite unhealthy. During the 1980s, Soviet leader Gorbachev introduced restrictions to wine importation in his effort to curb excess alcohol drinking. In just 3 years, Bulgarian exports to the Soviet Union dropped to 8 million barrels, which led to the uprooting of half of the Bulgarian vineyards (covering 4% of the country's territory). With privatization starting in 1990, Bulgarian wine has begun to make a comeback, although many of the traditional labels seem to have been neglected. A tendency toward pleasing the West European palette has been established, which international experts believe should be redirected toward improving the state of high quality local wines.

This chapter offers some brief notes on the most popular traditional alcohol drinks and some current wine labels. A number of other wines worth mentioning are the white Dimyat, the white Rkatsitely, the very light white Perla, the deep red Melnik, and the widely exported red Cabernet Sauvignon.

Grozdova Rakiya (Grape Brandy)
42 % alcohol brandy produced from grapes. Traditionally popular in southeastern Bulgaria.

Slivova Rakiya (Plum Brandy)
40 to 42 % alcohol. This seems to be the most popular traditional Bulgarian brandy especially in northeastern and western Bulgaria.

Plodova Rakiya (Fruit Brandy)
38 to 49 % alcohol. The Plodova Rakiya is produced predominantly from apricots.

Mentovka (Mint Liquer)
30 % alcohol. This is the only traditional Bulgarian liqueur.

Pelin (Worm-wood Wine)
Low alcohol (10.5 %) wine. Delightful, although unstable, wine which can be stored safely only until the spring after it is made.

Gumza (Red Gumza Grape Dry Wine)
13 % alcohol. This traditionally was one of the very popular wines from northern Bulgaria, produced from gumza grapes which at times have a very large yield. This

happens during high moisture years, resulting in a pallid, thin wine that oxidizes quickly.

During dry years when there is a lower yield of grapes, the gumza is a champion: it reveals its depth and discloses an unprecedented ability to age.

The Novo Sello winery, which produces this wine together with other wineries along the Danube and north of the Balkan range, takes pride in their 1930's record of the "all time highest degree of natural alcohol in a wine."

Trakiya (Dry Red Wine)

This is a Sliven region, 12 % alcohol, dry red wine made and bottled by "Vini" Sliven.

It is a full bodied wine, produced from the Cabernet Sauvignon grape used in the Bordeaux wines of France. The dry sunny climate and the sandy soil of the Sliven region in southeastern Bulgaria, where this wine comes from, are ideal for this red, full bouquet dry wine.

Exported by "Vinimpex," Sofia, it is imported in the USA by Monsieur Henri Wines, Ltd, White Plains, NY.

Menada (Red Wine)

12 % alcohol. Cellared and bottled by Menada winery and vineyards, this wine is produced from 61% Cabernet Sauvignon and 39% Merlot.

Although dry, its "Private Reserve," has a very light, pleasant flavor. It contains sulfites.

It comes from Oryachovitza in northern Bulgaria, one of the oldest wine-producing areas of Bulgaria. The label was established in 1901, and has recently been successfully restored.

Imported in the US by San Diego Impex, Carlsbad, California.

Mavrood (Red Mavrood Grape Dry Wine)

13% alcohol. According to world experts, this is the most unfairly treated Bulgarian wine. It has small berries, is hard to grow, and has a small yield. That is why most growers have not been enthusiastic about growing it. At the present there are only about 247 acres of it in the Assenovgrad area in south Bulgaria. (Compare that to the 62,000 acres in the champagne area of France!) Yet it is a priceless wine. In good years it reveals its qualities: Very deep colored, dense, heavy, tannic, and remarkably long lasting. French experts compare it with the Mouvedre from South France, favoring the Mavrud.[1]

Shefka (Rosé from Shefka and Local Muscat Grapes)

A wine of delicate flavor popular in the 1930s, it was produced by the Sliven "Shefka wineries," established in 1921. A 1 to 2 mixture between a very sweet local pink, dessert muscat grape (called "nashensky misket"), which has a very high tannin content, and very thick skin, and another local grape used for filling-in red wines, called "Shefka."

Sungurlare Muskat ("Sungurlare" dry white wine)

Containing 11.5 % vol. alcohol, this is a slightly fruity, yet very light white dry wine with crystal clarity. It too has been very popular since the 1930s, when it established its present-day label. It is a very old wine though, which has been produced in local southeastern Bulgarian wineries from local grapes since the ninteenth century.

It has been traditionally a 4 to 1 mixture. The basic grape was a white, high natural sugar, very large grape called "Bulgar." (Its name was given in the 1930s to replace its original middle-nineteenth-century Turkish name "Hafuz Ali.") The other ingredient is a very green, very thick skinned, and extremely aromatic local muscat grape called "Egipetsky misket" (Egyptian muscat).

---

1 The Mavrud is one of the 27 Bulgarian wines with the status of "controliran" label. That is a standard given to wines which for 3 years in a row have shown stable qualities. The "controliran" labels are checked very closely, and can be disqualified at any time.

A good present-day label is the "Sungarlare Muscat" vinted and bottled by "vinex Slaviantsi" winery, Bulgaria. Another "controliran" licensed label.

Index

Other Cookbooks of Interest
from Hippocrene ...

ALL ALONG THE DANUBE: Recipes from Germany, Austria, Czechoslovakia, Yogoslavia, Hungary, Romania, and Bulgaria
by Marina Polvay
For novices and gourmets, this unique cookbook offers a tempting variety of Central European recipes form the shores of the Danube River, bringing Old World flavor to today's dishes.
349pp • 5 ½ x 8 ½ • 0-7818-0098-6 • $14.95pb • (491)

BAVARIAN COOKING
by Olli Leeb
With over 300 recipes, this lovely collector's item cookbook covers every aspect of Bavarian cuisine from drinks, salads and breads to main courses and desserts.
"*Bavarian Cooking* is what a good regional cookbook should be—a guide for those who wish to know the heart and soul of a region's cooking, a book that anchors its recipes in the culture that produced them, and a cookbook that brings delight to the casu reader as well as to the serious cook." —*German Life*
176pp • 6 ½ x 8 ½ • 0-7818-0561-9 • $25.00hc • (659)

THE BEST OF CZECH COOKING
by Peter Trnka
Simple yet elegant recipes from this little-known cuisine.
230pp • 5 ½ x 8 ½ • 0-7818-0453-1 • $22.50hc • (551)
Paperback: 5 x 8 ½ • 0-7818-0492-2 • $12.95pb • (376)

THE ART OF HUNGARIAN COOKING, Revised Edition
by Paul Pogany Bennett and Velma R. Clark
Whether you crave Chicken Paprika or Apple Strudel, these 222 authentic Hungarian recipes include a vast array of national favorites, from appetizers through desserts. Now updated with a concise guide to Hungarian wines!
225pp • 5 ½ x 8 ½ • 18 b/w drawings • 0-7818-0586-4 • $11.95pb • (686)

POLISH HERITAGE COOKERY, Illustrated Edition
by Robert and Maria Strybel

New illustrated edition of a bestseller with 20 color photographs!
"An encyclopedia of Polish cookery and a wonderful thing to have!"
>—Julia Child, Good Morning America

"Polish Heritage Cookery is the best [Polish] cookbook printed in English on the market.
It's well-organized, informative, interlaced with historical background on Polish foods and
eating habits, with easy-to-follow recipes readily prepared in American kitchens and,
above all, it's fun to read." —Polish American Cultural Network

915pp • 6 x 9 • 16pp color photos • over 2,200 recipes
0-7818-0558-9 • $39.95hc • (658)

THE BEST OF POLISH COOKING
Revised Edition
by Karen West

"A charming offering of Polish cuisine with lovely woodcuts throughout."
—Publisher's Weekly
219pp • 5 ½ x 8 ½ • 0-7818-0123-3 • $8.95pb • (391)

OLD WARSAW COOKBOOK
by Rysia

Eight hundred fifty authentic and easy to prepare Polish recipes.
300pp • 5 x 7 ½ • 0-87052-932-3 • $12.95pb • (536)

OLD POLISH TRADITIONS
IN THE KITCHEN AND AT THE TABLE

A cookbook and a history of Polish culinary customs. Short essays cover subjects like
Polish hospitality, holiday traditions, even the exalted status of the mushroom. The recipes
are traditional family fare.
304pp • 5 x 8 ½ • 0-7818-0488-4 • $11.95pb • (546)

TASTE OF ROMANIA
by Nicolae Klepper

A real taste of both old world and modern Romanian culture. More than 140 recipes,
including the specialty dishes of Romania's top chefs, are intermingled with fables, poetry,
photos and illustrations in this comprehensive and well organized guide to Romanian
cuisine.
320pp • 5 ½ x 8 ½ • 0-7818-0523-6 • $24.95hc • (637)

THE CUISINE OF ARMENIA
by Sonia Uvezian

The definitive guide to creating the authentic flavors of Armenian food.
384pp • 5 ½ x 8 ½ • 0-7818-0417-5 • $14.95pb • (457)

Bulgarian Language Guide and Dictionaries . . .

BEGINNER'S BULGARIAN
207pp • 5 ½ x 8 ½ • 0-7818-0300-4 • $9.95pb • (76)

BULGARIAN-ENGLISH/ENGLISH-BULGARIAN PRACTICAL DICTIONARY
323pp • 4 ⅜ x 7 • 6,500 entries • 0-87052-145-4 • $14.95pb • (331)

BULGARIAN-ENGLISH/ENGLISH-BULGARIAN COMPACT DICTIONARY
323pp • 3 ½ x 4¾ • 6,500 entries • 0-7818-0535-X • $8.95pb • (623)

BULGARIAN-ENGLISH COMPREHENSIVE DICTIONARY
1,050pp • 6 ¾ x 9 ¾ • 47,000 entries • 0-7818-0507-4 • $90.00 2-vol set • (613)

ENGLISH-BULGARIAN COMPREHENSIVE DICTIONARY
1,080pp • 6 ¾ x 9 ¾ • 54,000 entries • 0-7818-0508-2 • $90.00 2-vol set • (614)